Love Secrets

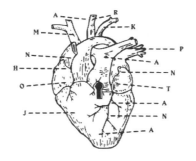

John Mark Pantana

HELLO.

Before you read the words that I've prepared for you: hello, my name is John Mark.

Let's air-high-five.

Hopefully, you actually did.

I have lots of little goodies in this book you're about to read. I pray that, even now, you can sense the sweetness of the Holy Spirit. May He illuminate your heart to the love of the Father and the beautiful, finished work of Jesus.

Also, you look nice today.

TABLE OF CONTENTS

HOW TO READ THIS BOOK

From left to right. That's the first step. The second is equally as important: *with a guarded heart.*

"The Bereans were open-minded in that they received the Word with all readiness and searched the Scriptures daily to find out whether these things were so" (Acts 17:11).

Open-minded but heart guarded. Don't fully accept my or anyone else's word for it. I received many popular Western teachings that bound me. The Bereans took what they heard and searched the Scriptures to *"find out whether these things were so."* This is good practice. Also, I believe the Holy Spirit will *"ring a bell"* within you, testifying to truth-that-sets-you-free.

Third step: expect to experience the person of Jesus. I have included *prompts* at the end of each chapter for you to engage the Father, Jesus, and the Holy Spirit in an experiential way. *With each prompt,* let *the eyes of your heart* open-wide for a fresh-wave of glory-enjoyment; this little practice can shake loose heaps of dormant head-knowledge. For a *real* knowledge, truth must be awakened in the heart. Just a few minutes of heart-connection with God could change your entire life. I've included blank *space for you* at the end of each chapter to write down anything that happens.

Fourth step: listen to music! This book is intrinsically linked to my music record: *Love Secrets;* thirteen songs about

God's love. And now: thirteen chapters. Each chapter of this book is titled after a song from the album and explores in detail the truths I sing about. I've arranged the order of chapters differently from the album for a more fluid reading experience. *I would recommend* listening to the corresponding song during the prompts at the end. You can listen to *Love Secrets* on every music platform.

Fifth and finally: have fun. You'll notice this book is not prim and proper. I hope you giggle and enjoy the goofy banter.

Book instructions complete.

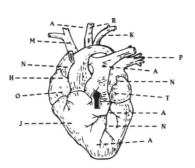

Chapter One

SWEETER THAN WINE

My family moved to the blue hills of Virginia when I was in the first grade. I attended Christian everything—*private school, church three times a week, youth group; even the businesses spoke in Christianese.* This microcosm had some benefits and also not-so-much. Hanging most vividly, on the line of dirty laundry, was the well-mannered works-based teaching. In my case, no one angrily yelled half-truths, but even a gentleman's lie will bear fruit unto death.

Words are *seeds.* Every word that we willingly *accept* in the soil of our hearts, we give permission to grow and bear fruit; whether that fruit is death or life always depends on the *substance* of the word. The words I accepted had an *appearance* of godliness but actually yielded death. Foul innards with a shiny aesthetic; like a gold-encrusted piece of poo.

Result: I sang in the choir, enjoyed the occasional spiritual goosebump, quoted chunks of passages from my dusty Bible, and thought God was a crass, old man. I squeaked the sinner's prayer thousands of times and walked the chapel aisle every week to get re-saved. *"Maybe this time it will work."* I became a closet atheist in a Christian home after walking the aisle one too many times. When my gold-covered-death-seeds came in for harvest, they pushed my heart happily away from God.

At the age of 14, I dropped out of Christian school and plunged into a five-year video game addiction; 16 hours a day was *normal.* I stopped developing emotionally, socially, and spiritually. I hated every waking moment when not attached like a parasite to my digital-dopamine-screen. You know, those grungy gamers living in their mom's basement? Yeah—*that was me.*

The only time I would dare leave my dungeon was for Sunday lunch. My big Italian family poured in for mom's homemade meals; brothers, sisters, droves of nieces and nephews, mom and pops. *The whole gang.* I was awkwardly just *there.* I engaged as much as a hermit could, but everyone sounded like Charlie Brown—*mumbling.* After scarfing a few plates, the withdrawals would beckon me back to my dungeon chair.

One particular Sunday, though, my brother's booming voice cut through, and I overheard, *"This preacher's been getting kicked out of churches for preaching the Gospel."* I pretended to pay no attention, but inwardly I thought, *"Getting kicked out of churches? I might listen to that guy."*

I listened. This was the *"gospel"* that I heard—*If God was real, then He was mad, and I was screwed.* Ironically, the word gospel renders *"too good to be true news."* This time around, the man speaking actually was angry. And, man, did he make God out to be angry too. This was like my conservative Christian school chapel but on a serious amount of crack. As a dog returns to his vomit, I PTSD'ed right back into a slavish fear of God, and that same-old aisle-walking-choirboy came out from hiding. The next day: I filed for divorce with my five-year computer-marriage, moved out of my mom's basement, and began suffering chronic dopamine withdrawals. I had the capacity of the average pre-teen at the age of 19. Also, I was *nerdy and awkward.*

Fear is a *great* motivator and can move any man to action if you heap it on thick enough—*it motivated me out of my dungeon.* Many communicators use fear-and-or-guilt tactics because of their quick, grabby effects on listeners. These microwaved results are deemed repentance. Sadly though, fear holds absolutely no power to change the human heart or produce healthy relationship. I enrolled in Christian college, *officially* more afraid of God than ever before. Little did I know I had left one taskmaster for another.

For the next three years, I crashed-and-burned up and down in a fear-based relationship with God. High highs and low lows. More of the same Spirit-less, works-centric, confusing Christianity. I pleaded daily with God to mold me into someone He deemed acceptable. I thought perhaps at any moment He'd strike me dead or slip me some cancer for my constant failure. I grew to *hate* the Christian life.

In all my accountability groups, confession sessions, Bible-reading, theology wars, worship leading—*I found no abundant life and no acceptance with God.* I desired to be free but found no ability and no help to get to Freedom's evasive Promise Land. I was stuck in unwanted addiction, along with every other honest Christian I had ever talked to.

The most torturous part of my lifeless religion was the screaming conscience—*guilty!* Out of genuineness, I left the faith, the church, and my dysfunctional relationship with God for the second time at the age of 22. For the next two years, I attempted to quiet my conscience, but it stubbornly kept demanding someone pay for my sins. In response, I wake-and-baked with some big-fat-tokes on my tubular-glass-bong, affectionately named *The Kraken.* My steady, all-day high coupled well with a heavy diet of *pornography and cigarettes.*

I would curse your socks off if you killed my buzz with conversation about God. He was, after all, the most abusive person in my jaded belief system. I earned my bachelor's at a *Christian University* under the influence; that was the *only* miracle I witnessed. Stoned and cynical, I pawned everything that didn't fit in my 1998 granny-wagon and said goodbye to the bible-belt for the first time at the age of 24.

I landed in the flatlands of the Midwest, and God was waiting for me there in the Wal-Mart parking lot. A Spirit-filled preacher barreled through my car speakers: *"God wants to show Himself to you. Call Him Dad!"* Every cell in my body was standing on the edge of their seat. I think heaven might have been too.

For the first time in my overwhelmingly-Christian-filled life, I cried out to God, *"Dad!"* The Holy Spirit rushed my vehicle and hugged my neck like the Father hugged the prodigal son—*with many kisses.* God's heart was radically different than I thought; infinite levels of kindness-singing-dancing-happy type of different. He was so proud of me; He could barely contain Himself. He belly-laughed in joyous thunder at the thought of me—*His son.* He knew my every corridor and still *fully* accepted me. He was my Father, and I was His son, and that's all there was to it.

Like dust settling in a room, I came back to reality and thought, *"Wait a second. You've got the wrong guy, God. I suck, remember?"* The foundation in my castle of man-made theology had just *cracked.* Like an abused puppy, I reservedly enjoyed the affection, but couldn't fully rest having never felt a Master's loving touch.

Before, when I heard people tell me God was loving, I thought they were just hippy-loving, tree-huggers. I wondered, *"What about sin?"* It was this loud sin on my conscience that always inhibited me from receiving God's love. Whenever love was mentioned, I quickly contorted, *"but He's also Holy."* In true religious fashion: *I knew little holiness or intimacy with God.* Sometimes, the loudest voices for God's holiness have the loudest guilty conscience.

For the next three years, my plastic castle melted as the Holy Spirit unveiled the Gospel of Grace. *"Jesus became sin, who knew no sin, that we might become the righteousness of God in Christ"* (2 Cor. 5:21). This verse lightning-bolted my heart. Jesus became sin on the Cross and received its full wage. All that I deserve: *Jesus received.* My *conscience* had always demanded a sin-payment, and I continually offered *myself* as the sacrifice. I had been entering God's kitchen with freshly roasted, self-righteous, grade-A flesh, insulting the Lamb He had already set and prepared for me to enjoy. The *entirety* of my Christian life was spent trying to pay for a sin-debt that had already been paid in full and finish a work that Christ emphatically said is *"Finished."* When Jesus cried those words, *"It is finished!"*, it beautifully meant, *"We will pay the wages of sin."* His choice of *"we"* reveals a mystery: *"the Father was reconciling the world to Himself in Christ, not counting people's sins against them"* (2 Cor. 5:19). The Father probably has holes in His hands too.

The Father, in Christ, did such a perfect job of removing our sins that the Holy Spirit, our Advocating Attorney, now witnesses to us, *"God will by no means count your sins against you or ever remember your lawless deeds"* (Heb. 10:17). That's quite different than what I thought the Spirit was kin to: *"A nagging wife is like water going drip-drip-drip on a rainy day"* (Prov. 27:15). Fault-finder-gut-grinder. While we tend to interact with the Spirit as the ghost-of-sinful-past, His main ministry is convincing us of forever-forgiveness. David prophetically spoke of this, saying, *"Blessed is the one whose sin the Lord will never count against them"* (Rom. 4:8). This blessed person is not blessed because they don't sin, but rather, because their sin is *never* counted against them.

While the Father, Jesus, and the Holy Spirit were fully satisfied and convinced of my innocence, *I had never been.* I found more air-tight evidence: God would now consider Himself *unjust* to condemn me for a sin Christ has already paid for. Heaven's Courts agree the same crime cannot be tried twice. While the Old Covenant says, *"God will by no means clear the guilty"* (Exod. 34:7), Jesus presents a new reality where God is *righteous* in calling the sinner righteous (Rom. 4:5). The Cross triumphantly calls God's justice as your legal defense, and there is absolutely no case against you. *"Who dares accuse us? No one—for God Himself has given us right standing with Himself. Who then will condemn us?"* (Rom. 8:33-34).

Being rooted in Christ's payment for sin is a very real weapon in your hand. I was constantly accused by my own guilty conscience and by the demonic, *"You think God will hear you? You are a terrible Christian! You are guilty!"* This is when you point your conscience and the devil to the Cross— *"There is my punishment!"* Although the accusation might be correct according to your failure, you dare not accept the guilt or punishment for something that has already been paid. Your acceptance of sin's punishment reeks of *unbelief* in the work of Christ. By ignoring the Cross and accepting condemnation, you empower the cycle of addiction and embrace the ministry of death. Condemnation kills the physical and emotional realm with cellular civil war.

It is tempting to the flesh to *pay the wages* with subtle, self-righteous behaviors: Hail Marys, helping little old ladies across the street, groveling in the dirt, church, inflicting self-pain, tithing, distancing from God, humanitarian aid, self-hatred, and so on. We tend to try and settle this sin-debt on our guilty conscience with either behavior, *(that's called dead works)*, or self-punishment, when only the Cross has the power to *free* the conscience from demanding payment for sin. When you try to *pay the wages* in these ways, you have not allowed your conscience to be *satisfied* with the blood of Christ. The eyes of your heart *must* see sin's wages being fully paid by Christ in your stead. If you *rest* in what Christ has done, just like the angels declaring glad tidings of *"Peace, from God, towards men,"* every cell in your body will cry *"Peace."*

Jesus received our sin at the Cross, took it to the grave, and left it *all* behind when He rose. The Father, by the power of the Holy Spirit, would not have raised Jesus from the dead if our sins had not been fully put away. His resurrection is proof of your perfect innocence. Our living Lord is a receipt.

If we stopped there, that would be *good news*. But there's another side to the coin. All that Jesus is: *"so am I in this world"* (1 John 4:17). In the same way that Jesus received our sin, we *receive* His very own righteousness as our own. This beautiful exchange was foretold in the Old Covenant sin offering. In the Old Covenant, when you sinned, you brought a lamb to your local priest. The priest did *not* inspect you; he inspected the lamb. It was obvious why you were there—*you sinned.* If the lamb was deemed perfect, you placed your hands on this *"animal without blemish"* as it breathed its last. It was taught that in this moment, your sin was imputed to the lamb, and the lamb's righteousness was imputed to you. *"Behold, the Lamb of God, who takes away the sin of the world!"* (John 1:29).

Christ is our lamb. We have *"placed our hands"* on Him and traded our sin for His perfect righteousness. This means His very own righteousness has been deposited in our account. Take a moment and think about the ramifications of this provision: we are *equally* as righteous as Christ because Jesus, Himself, *is* our righteousness. *"Christ has become to you righteousness"* (1 Cor. 1:30). The Scriptures pin the Gospel with this righteous reality, *"For in the Gospel the righteousness of God is revealed—a righteousness that is by faith"* (Rom. 1:17). Notice the Gospel, very specifically, reveals the righteousness of God *received* by faith. The Good News does not reveal man's sinfulness or man's righteousness; it reveals Christ alone—*our gifted righteousness.*

In the Old Covenant, righteousness was *earned.* In the New Covenant, righteousness is *received.* One is merited, and one is unmerited. These are *opposite* frequencies. The reason that *"the Law is not based on faith"* (Gal. 3:12) is because faith *receives*, it does not earn. It is when you attempt to *earn* what cannot be earned, that you forfeit the free gift. *"You have fallen from Grace you who attempt to be justified by the Law of Moses"* (Gal. 5:4). Notice falling from Grace is not outward sin, but rather, attempting to be righteous via behavior.

Jesus drew close and healed prostitutes, but the religious who were known for their good deeds, stood at a distance and *never* received from Him. Gifted-righteousness shames man-glory and calls self-righteousness filthy rags. Paul comments on this: *"For they being ignorant of God's righteousness, and seeking to establish their own righteousness, have not submitted to the righteousness of God. For Christ is the end of the Law for righteousness to everyone who believes"* (Rom. 10:3-4).

We've just looked at two sides of the same coin—*sin and righteousness*. Jesus received your sin, and you receive His righteousness. For your sake and convincing, God has laid this judicially-sound foundation at the Cross. Let your conscience be settled that God, Himself, has promised He will *never* count your sins against you. Stand your ground in the gifted *"breastplate of righteousness"* Christ has provided for you to wear. God is no longer inspecting you for righteousness. He's inspecting your *offering*. Are you confident that Christ is in right-standing with God? Use that *same confidence* to believe you are in equal standing! This means as your *confidence* in Christ grows, so does your *confidence* with God.

Christ's *finished* work on the Cross is the foundation of the Gospel, and every additional layer in the Christian life must be built, precept upon precept, upon this solid rock. His *"Finished"* is our starting point. These glad tidings of great joy remove every excuse and every hindrance rudely standing in opposition to real intimacy with God. Paul said it this way: *"Not having my own righteousness, which is from the Law, but a righteousness which is through faith in Christ; that I may know Him"* (Phil. 3:9-10). Notice the result of gifted righteousness: *"that I may know Him."* This Christ-foundation is to swing wide the doors of intimacy. With such great security, your heart can be free. You have an anchor now, regardless of ups and downs, that stays fixed and steady—*Christ Himself.*

It is time to let yourself be loved for Goodness sake and get to *know* God. Arkansas was my wilderness, but I met God there. With the Gospel's permission, I cozied up *real* close to God. I had been longing for this *permission* my entire life. From age 24 to 27, I drank in His affection all-day-every-day in true monk-status. I tasted and saw that He is *very good.*

Fast-forward and I've just opened the door to mom's basement—*the old dungeon.* I was hoteling there. I had left the Midwest at the leading of the Holy Spirit for a house church back in my hometown. The first morning in that *old-addiction-dungeon*, I woke up to a sweet, still voice, *"Do you believe My love is better than life?"* Half-asleep, I mumbled, *"Yes, Lord,"* and moseyed to breakfast; oops—*not very spiritual.* Again, He asked, *"Do you believe My love is better than life?"* I said, *"Yes, of course, Lord."* Nom, nom, nom. And a third time, He asked, *"Do you believe My love is better than life?"* The sweetness of the Holy Spirit rested on me. My eyes watering and my heart fully attentive, I began worshiping: *"I believe You love me. Your love is better than life. Your love is sweeter than wine."*

This simple moment of worship is when the Jesus-music started flooding in. It was only later I realized the Lord was quoting, *"Because your love is better than life, my lips will glorify you"* (Psalm 63:3). Rooted in the Gospel of Grace, conscience free, and heart stable: *I believe God loves me.*

PROMPTS

Free The Conscience

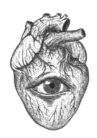

A seared conscience is being *"perpetually conscious of sins,"* which leads to restrictive teachings like forbidding to marry and abstaining from food (1 Tim. 4:2). An obsessive focus on sin—*both to sin and to not sin*—is the sign of a seared conscience. This seared conscience has not been perfected by the Cross and typically creates cultures of legalism.

The Law demands payment for sin and *sears* the conscience. The Gospel provides payment for sin and *frees the conscience*. Whereas the Old Covenant sacrifices were a reminder of sins, Christ's sacrifice is meant to perfect the human conscience with *"no more consciousness of sin"* (Heb. 10:2). God has designed one thing to free your conscience from demanding payment: *The Cross.*

Jesus was punished by the Romans, beaten to the point that His bones laid bare. His treatment was so foul that *"He was unrecognizable."* Pinned to a tree by thick nails, He absorbed and suffered sin's consequence—*death*. The wages of sin are death and He paid death's entire tab compelled by a passionate desire to provide your *freedom*.

Picture this loving Man on the Cross. Hear Him yelling, *"Finished!"* which renders: *"We will pay the wages for sin."* Let your conscience be satisfied with Him paying for *all* your wrongs. You don't have to pay the wages or punish yourself anymore. You can *cease* your civil war. Take a few minutes to do this. Close your eyes, and with the eyes of your heart, behold Jesus on the Cross.

Selah.

Selah means to take a moment and connect your heart to God. I'll use this word during the prompts at good points for you to chill out, focus off the book, and onto Jesus.

SPACE FOR YOU

If God speaks, you should write.

LYRICS

Listen to: Sweeter Than Wine

I believe you love me
I believe you care for me

Your love is better than life
Your love is sweeter than wine
Your love is better than life
Your love is sweeter than the sweetest wine

Even on my worst day
You were right there with me

Chapter Two

THIS IS LOVE

Prior to Grace, you could sum up my Christian life in this: *my love for God*. That doesn't sound too bad, but our love for God is not the Good News. *Our* love for God is actually the summation of the Old Covenant.

"What is the greatest commandment?" When Jesus answered this question posed by the religious leaders of His day, He quickly summed the Old Covenant with, *"You shall love the Lord your God with all your heart, with all your soul, and with all your mind. This is the first and greatest commandment. And the second is like it: You shall love your neighbor as yourself. On these two commandments hang all the Law and the Prophets"* (Matt. 22:37-40). Do you see all these *"your"* statements?

The Law's message is clear: *you should love God and love people.* And yet, Corinthians indicts the Law *"written and engraved on stones"* as the *"ministry of death"* and *"ministry of condemnation."* Romans says that the Law is just, holy, and good, but is powerless because of *"sinful flesh"* in helping us do what it demands. Its perfection is our very *problem.*

Hey, ladies. You're shopping for a new dress; a yellow, summer dress. Why not? Giddy with excitement, you try it on in the dressing room. You turn and look in the mirror. *"Oh, no!"* This dress does not agree with you. Just think of it this way: it can't handle you—*literally.* What a rude, rude dress this is. Now, whose fault is this? More specifically: is this the mirror's fault?

I know you want to punch the mirror, but really, the mirror is innocent. It's simply showing you what's going on with *you.* This mirror cannot bend in its absolute perfection of showing you, *you!* This mirror has no heart of love to offer you sweet nothings in your ear despite your yellow-dress-mess. That's not the purpose of a mirror.

The Law is this mirror. It shows you what's up with your flesh. In all of its full glory and perfection, it shines unbendingly upon your adherence to its commands! It cannot bend one millimeter, or it would forfeit its glorious perfection as **LAW.** Though it demands wonderful things, it offers no support and lends no aid. You are simply left with you and your ability to *perform.*

Perform for the Law, and you'll stand condemned every-single-time. Live under Law, and you might as well tattoo: 1) guilty or 2) self-righteous on your forehead; which way you swing depends on how much stiff-necked pride you have. Preach the Law, and you'll *revive* sin. *"For apart from the*

16

Law, sin was dead. I was alive once without the Law, but when the commandment came, sin revived, and I died" (Rom. 7:8b-9). This verse is memorized in hell for some good ole' fashioned sin-revivals. Many good-intentioned believers are killing their listeners, and empowering sin, with zealous ignorance of the Law's purpose. *"The strength of sin is the Law"* (1 Cor. 15:56). If sin is fire, the Law is gasoline. This is why Romans pins the Law's purpose to *"make all men guilty before God"* and the obvious conclusion that *"no flesh will be justified in God's sight by the Law."* This flesh-pointing mirror was a taskmaster—*an inflexible tutor meant to exhaust our pride.*

"All that you command of us, we can do!" This is the heart of what Israel said to God before the Law was given. The Hebrew language renders this as drenched in pride. *"We'd rather relate to you based our own goodness, God."* For the first time in Israel's grace-ridden history, God promoted distance; *"Don't come near the mountain lest you die."*

We were *never* meant to relate to God according to righteousness that comes from the Law. Paul always communicated this reality: *"not having my own righteousness which is from the Law."* Please notice that righteousness earned from the Law is *self-righteousness*. This means the righteousness the Law demands must be earned *without* help. Paul goes on to say he would consider his Law-righteousness dung compared to *"a righteousness from faith,"* which is gifted righteousness from God (Phil. 3:9-10).

This is why Jesus elevated the holiness standard of the Law to the Pharisees who thought they were in right-standing with God, based on their adherence to the Law. *"You have heard that it was said, 'You shall not commit adultery.' But I say to you that whoever looks at a woman to lust for her has*

17

already committed adultery with her in his heart" (Matt. 5:27-28). Imagine seeing peepy-Joe's face when he heard Jesus say that. There goes his heavenly-pension. *"Who can be made right with God if this is so?"*

An inward coming-to-the-end-of-your-self-rope must happen before a total reliance on Christ for all things begins. The Law, in all its unbending glory, will snap any rope. When it does, it has tutored us *well* unto Christ. How sweet to taste the glad-tidings of restful Grace when we've *hard-slogged* to earn it *by the sweat of our brow* for so long.

The Ten Commandments, which Jesus summarized in two, are the foundation of the Law and are, in essence, *"Do these good things and don't do these evil things."* This is simply the knowledge of good and evil. Remind you of a tree?

God said, *"you will surely die"* if you eat from the Tree of the Knowledge of Good and Evil. This tree represents the Law for *"the letter kills"* (2 Cor. 3:6). It was when Adam ate the Law that his conscience awoke to sin because *"by the Law is the knowledge of sin"* (Rom. 3:20). Which tree you eat from determines if you'll have the knowledge of sin or the knowledge of Christ.

God continually sets these two trees before us today. Will you eat from the Law or from Life? When I ate from the Old Tree: *I wallowed in death and knew nothing of intimacy.* (Adam used to walk with God but hid after he ate.) *"Who told you that you were naked?"* Adam's conscience, freshly seared by the Law, said, *"Guilty!"* Just like Adam, my Christian-normal was a repetitive cycle of failing, guilt for it, fig-leaf distancing, and finally shame. Shame is identifying with sin *instead* of Christ.

Add up all these indictments, and it is obvious why *God* found fault with the first Covenant (Heb. 8:7). The will of the Father that Jesus completed was to *"Set aside the first [Covenant] to establish the second"* (Heb. 10:9). Much of my confusion came from prominent Western voices that taught (and sang) as if Jesus didn't change or accomplish anything. *Old-Tree-Syndrome.*

Perhaps you don't have peace with God because you've been hearing a weak mixture of these Covenants your whole life. *"God's love is unconditional. Except it has lots of conditions."* Jesus said when you patch an old wineskin with new skins, both break, and both lose their power. He'd prefer Covenants be hot or cold—*not mixed at lukewarm.* Mixing Law with Grace, which some call balance, spoils both. Castrate the Law by bending its perfection, and it will never snap a self-righteous rope. Add a little leaven of the Law to Grace and dim the glory of Christ. You could say it this way: If God wants all the glory, let Him do *all* the work.

Jesus changed everything, including our Covenant with God, and it's a far superior Covenant, built on better promises (Heb. 8:6). Prophesied by Jeremiah, and repeated by the author of Hebrews, God says, *"For this is the [new] Covenant that I will make with the house of Israel says the LORD: I will put My desires on their hearts; and I will be their God, and they shall be My people"* (Heb. 8:10). Do you see all these *"I"* statements from God?

This New Covenant is focused solely on God's behavior *towards us.* It doesn't look like we have much of a role to play here. How do we enter this New Covenant? *"For I will be merciful to their unrighteousness, and their sins and their lawless deeds I will remember no more"* (Heb. 8:12). The Greek in this verse communicates: *"I promise with all that I am, I will absolutely never count your wrongs against you. May it never be!"* This is a double-clad guarantee. Our entry into this much-better Covenant is through God's actions, not ours. Our role is simply to believe the glad tidings of God's love *for* us. Whereas the Old Covenant could be summed up by our love *for* God, the New Covenant is summed up by God's love *for* us.

Scene: A motley crew of Jewish-Seminary rejects have been kicking it with their rogue Rabbi for three years. They've seen, time after time, this Jesus, *"anointed with the Holy Ghost and with power doing good and healing all that were oppressed of the devil"* (Acts 10:38). Jesus, overcoming death everywhere He goes, has mentioned His own death quite a few times over the years. His disciples, unlearned fishermen, let it go in one ear and out the other. *"Stop talking crazy, Jesus."*

Before Jesus' death, He calls for one last supper, telling Peter and John, *"Go and prepare the Passover for us, that we may eat"* (Luke 22:8). Our two boys, Peter and John, are about to provide a fitting contrast at this dinner party. Jesus drops the bomb again. *"My blood will be shed for you."* Peter, whose name renders *stone (Law)*, responds in true strong-willed fashion, *"Lord, I am ready to go with You, both to prison and to death"* (Luke 22:33). John, whose name renders *Grace*, makes no boast and rests his head on Jesus' chest. The disciple boasting in *his* love for God ends up denying Him three times. The disciple resting on Jesus' heart of love ends up at the foot of the Cross during His crucifixion. The Law births bondage. Grace bears fruit to God.

John's affectionate title, *"the disciple whom Jesus loved,"* only appears in John's own writings. This disciple, who had no special access to Jesus compared to his peers, simply leaned all of his weight on the love of Christ *for* him. Believing and living this way will produce in you a beautiful intimacy with God. Peter, who felt distant from Jesus and most likely unsure of himself, had to ask John the Beloved for inside information at the Last Supper. *"John, can you ask Him for me, who is the betrayer? Is it me?"* Peter felt distance. John felt His heartbeat.

Our capacity to love God and love people is only as potent as our consent to receive His love for us. *"We love because He first loved us"* (1 John 4:19). Jesus put it simply and profoundly, *"As you have freely received, freely give."* Strap your receivers on, folks. God is constantly surveying the earth for a heart open to receive His inexhaustible affection. *"This is love: not that we love God, but that He loves us"* (1 John 4:10). You are the beloved, after all. Perhaps it's time to start posturing yourself as the *be-loved.*

OLD VS NEW

If you look in the Bible, there are two covenants.

Rightly dividing truth requires us to discern between Old and New. Many are zealous for God but live in a perpetual state of missing God's heart for a lack of this knowledge (Romans 10:2). This even happened to John the Beloved: *"Lord, should we call down fire from heaven and destroy them?"* (Luke 9:54). This is John's response to a town that collectively refused Jesus. Jesus, unoffended, rebuked fire-and-brimstone-John, saying, *"You do not know what manner of spirit you are of"* (Luke 9:55). John probably side-tilted his head in confusion. He was attempting to mimic Elijah, one of the Old Testament's most famed prophets. Jesus rebuked this well-intentioned mimicry. *Awkward.*

Old Covenant mimes zealously operate in the wrong spirit and wrong covenant. That's when you eat the meat and spit out all the bones. You need to be equipped to know the difference between Old and New and stop blindly accepting a lukewarm mixture. Luckily, the Holy Spirit loves guiding us into the full-fat, unadulterated truth. To help rightly discern Old and New, I have listed a few of my favorite paradigm-shifting-contrasts in the following pages.

The Old Covenant was given by **Moses**, a servant.
The New Covenant came by **Jesus Christ**, the Son.

———

The Old Covenant is **Law**.
The New Covenant is **Grace**.

———

The Law **demands**.
Grace **supplies**.

———

The Law **demands righteousness** in your actions.
Grace **supplies righteousness** as a gift to receive.

———

Under Law, our attire is **stained as filthy rags**.
Under Grace, we are **clothed in Christ's righteousness**.

———

Under Law, you're **defined in Adam**.
Under Grace, you're **defined in Christ**.

———

The Law is a mirror that **reflects your performance**.
Grace is a mirror that reflects your **identity in Christ**.

———

Under Law, **no flesh will be justified** in God's sight.
Under Grace, all who believe are **justified freely**.

———

The Law is **by works.**
Grace is **by faith**.

Under Law, **sacrifices were a reminder of sins**.
Under Grace, Jesus' sacrifice is meant to perfect the
conscience with **"no more consciousness of sins."**

———

The Law **points you to your sin**, for *"by the Law is the
knowledge of sin."*
The Holy Spirit **points you to Jesus** because, as we behold
Him, we become like Him.

———

Under Law, the **wages of sin is death**.
Under Grace, Jesus said, *"Finished"* at the Cross, which
renders **"We will pay the wages."**

———

Law is **obedience to the Law**; right *doing*.
Grace is **obedience to the Faith**; right *believing*.

———

The Law operates by the **flesh** (self-effort).
Grace operates by the **Spirit** (God-effort).

———

The Law was given on **Mount Sinai**.
The Spirit was given on **Mount Zion**.

———

The Law is the **strength of sin**.
Grace is the **power over sin**.

———

The Law is **helpless and powerless** to help man.
Grace **teaches us to deny all ungodliness**.

The Law demands, *"Do not commit adultery."*
Grace supplies the desire, wisdom, passion, love, and
faithfulness of Jesus.

———

The Law says, *"Do not steal."*
Grace creates a real, inward *generosity*.

———

The Law says, *"Love God with everything!"*
Grace says, *"This is love: not that we love God, but that **He
loves us.**"*

———

The Law says, *"Give to God!"* and He responds.
Grace says, *"God has given all!"* and we respond.

———

The Law says, *"Love your neighbor as yourself."*
Grace says, *"We love because Christ first loved us."*

———

The Law *cannot lift a finger to help* what it demands.
Grace *supplies both the desire and the ability* to do His good
pleasure.

———

The Law is a *cold tablet of stone*.
Grace is a *living, breathing, loving Person*.

———

The Law *has no fingers* to lend a hand.
Grace has *10 fingers and two hands of love*.

The Law was just a *type and shadow*.
Grace, the person of Christ, is the *substance*.

———

Under Law, *the letter kills*.
Under Grace, *the Spirit gives life*.

———

The Law *ministers death* via condemnation.
Grace *ministers life* via the Spirit.

———

The first miracle under Law, Aaron's rod of judgment turned
water into blood in a desert.
The first miracle under Grace, Jesus turned *water into wine* at
a wedding.

———

When the Law was given, 3000 *people died*.
When the Spirit was given, 3000 *people were saved*.

———

Cain brought the *"the works of his hands"* and was rejected.
Abel brought the *"the lamb"* and was accepted.

———

Abel's blood cried *vengeance*.
Jesus' blood cries *forgiveness*.

———

Under Law, sins are a *curse in family lines* up to the fourth
generation (Deut. 5:9).
Under Grace, *Christ became a curse on the Cross and
redeemed us from **all curses of the Law**.*

Under Law, you *work for your wages*.
Under Grace, you *inherit by blood*.

———

Under Law, *blessing is earned* by works.
Under Grace, *blessing is received* by faith.

———

Under Law, the promises of God are contingent upon *"If you obey all the commandments."*
Under Grace, the promises of God, in Christ, are *"Yes"* from God and *"Amen"* from you.

———

Under Law, obey, or *be cursed*.
Under Grace, *you are blessed* by Christ's obedience.

———

The Law is a brash tutor, *correcting with fear* of punishment.
The Holy Spirit is our Counselor, *correcting with Fatherly-words* and relationship.

———

God will *not help you* minister the Law.
God will *make you sufficient* to minister Grace.

———

Under Law, *who can know the Lord?*
Under Grace, *we have the mind of Christ*.

———

Under Law, Isaiah *lacked boldness* when he saw God.
Under Grace, we have *supreme boldness* to enter God's throne room by the blood of Jesus.

Under Law, **the devil had borrowed authority** on the earth given to him by Adam.
Under Grace, **Jesus legally reclaimed all authority** for man at the Cross having *"disarmed all principalities."*

———

Under Law, you **had no authority**.
Under Grace, you **share the authority** of King Jesus.

———

Under Law, David pleaded with God not to take the **Holy Spirit that was upon him**.
Under Grace, our spirit has been fused-married as **one spirit with the Lord**.

———

Under Law, the Spirit of God dwelled in the innermost part of the temple: **The Holy of Holies**.
Under Grace, the Spirit of God dwells in the innermost part of man: **the human spirit**.

———

Under Law, **intimacy cannot exist** with no security.
Under Grace, you need to **get a room.**

PROMPTS

Cast Out The Bondwoman

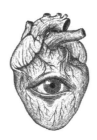

"You who desire to be under the Law, do you not hear the Law? Abraham had two sons: one by a bondwoman and the other by a freewoman. Ishmael was born according to the flesh and Isaac through promise which things are symbolic. These are the two Covenants and the one from Mount Sinai gives birth to bondage, which is Hagar. Nevertheless, what does the Scripture say? 'Cast out the bondwoman and her son, for Ishmael shall not be heir with Isaac'" (Gal. 4:21-24, 30).

These verses contrast Sarah and Hagar as the two Covenants—*Law and Grace.* God promised Abraham a son through his lawful wife, Sarah. After many years of waiting, Abraham took matters into his own hands and tried to fulfill God's promise by sleeping with his maid. Hagar, the mistress, bore Abraham a son named Ishmael; however, this birth was not by faith in God's promise. Hagar was still naturally able to have children. *"I can do this without believing God for it. I'm capable."* Although that may be true, this is practically how we live under the Old Covenant; doing things in our own strength

29

and timing without believing God for it. *"The Law is not based on faith"* (Gal. 3:12).

You *can* see results living under the Law. Ishmael *was* born. These results are contingent on man's might, strength, and power. The Scripture calls this *"flesh."* These results will only last for so long and eventually *"give birth to bondage."* The new way of living is *"by my Spirit, says the Lord"* (Zech. 4:6). Sarah, Abraham's lawful wife, also eventually bore Abraham a son, Isaac; this birth was by faith in God's promise. Sarah was well past the natural age of childbearing and her son's conception required supernatural help. God must do all the work under Grace. We just *believe*.

After Isaac was born, Sarah told Abraham, *"Cast out the bondwoman and her son!"* Since Hagar and Sarah represent the two Covenants, this is Grace pleading with you to cast out the Law and its fruit of self-effort. Just from this story you can see that the Law, practically, depends on man's effort while Grace depends on God's effort. The Scriptures goes on to say: *"Ishmael, the son of the bondwoman, shall not be heir with Isaac, the son of the freewoman!"* Who is your birth mother? Sarah or Hagar? You are an heir of God by Grace, not effort. Who is mothering you in life? Sarah or Hagar? The fruit of your life should birth from faith, not effort.

Take a moment, connect your heart to God, and ask, *"Where am I still believing or living in the Old Covenant?"* Release everything bringing you under bondage. Cast out the bondwoman!

Selah.

SPACE FOR YOU

Write, draw, compile grocery lists.

LYRICS

Listen to: This Is Love

This is love not that we love God
But that He loves us

We're the beloved
We're the beloved
We're the beloved of God

We love, we love because
He first loved us

Chapter Three

ON YOUR MIND

The night was Halloween, and I was trying to impress the cool kids at a local rock concert. Fresh off some heavy World of Warcraft withdrawals, I was offered my first cigarette at 19 years old. Three years later and I was smoking two packs of Cowboy Killers per day. When I left the faith, for the second time, at the age of 22—*I wanted to intentionally middle-finger God.* I thought, *"Might as well go for the gold."*

After a few violent upchucks, I was pretty much done with alcohol. Pot, on the other hand—*yeah, I kind of became the poster child.* I loved it. I rocked a hand-woven Rasta beanie and my gnarly, bare-feet twenty-four-seven. I laughed in disbelief, for ten minutes, the first time my THC-brain flavor-enhanced an entire bag of Krispy Kreme donuts. Add in neural-pathway-movies that combust with good music and this addict-prone, god-hating, white-boy was sold. For a solid two years, I was high as a kite.

I would highly recommend *not* smoking—*cigarettes or otherwise*. The pot-head John Mark would read that recommendation, roll his glassy-eyes, and blankety-blank you. *"I'd recommend you shove that unsolicited advice up your you-know-what, Captain."* Let's press pause.

Zoom in on my stoned, squinty eyes and behind them was literally tens-of-thousands of Christian sermons on behavior and surrender—*the two pillars of being a good Christian*. Name any famous, prominent voice for Christianity in America, and I had devoured their content with *no* lasting change. The only fruit it birthed in my heart was *shame*. I tried to behave and couldn't. And I could not, with good conscience, surrender to an untrustworthy God.

Every well-intentioned pulpit-plea only put the focus more squarely on *me*. The more I beheld me, the more I was *not* transformed, and the more God felt disappointed in me. This overwhelming focus on how I ought to live only made me more aware of my obvious dysfunction and of God's heavy disapproval. Not a thousand sermons on behavior or surrender could produce the very thing they called for. I thought myself an unrighteous bastard—*and so my actions followed*.

In the middle of my open rebellion, while I thought God a rude, old Man with a hard nature—*His thoughts towards me were good.* He had *not* distanced Himself one inch from my hot mess; I was on His mind even on my darkest day.

"Before He made the world, God had already chosen us to be His through our union with Christ and without fault in His eyes" (Eph. 1:4). I believe His Fathering heart is

provoked by our rebellion, but only to *compassion*. His affections are set on us. He intercedes for our awakening to His very nearness.

It wasn't until the root of my *beliefs* changed that I began to change. The foundation of my wrong-believing was that righteousness ebbed-and-flowed with my behavior. This foundation is sinking sand, constantly shifting, providing no solid ground to build our Christian life on. I continually beheld *myself* in the mirror of the Law, which, by its unbending nature, only revealed my inadequacy. This mirror communicates: *you are what you do!*

I then began beholding myself in the mirror of Christ, who, by His nature, revealed my perfect righteousness in Him. Where the Law had demanded righteousness in my behavior, Christ, liberally, and lovingly, provided Himself as my righteousness. This mirror communicates: *as Christ is, so are you!*

I celebration-dance-partied on my couch the first time my heart fully received the good news. I could finally *rest* from all my efforts. And like a trumpet blast, Jesus' *"It is finished!"* echoed through my weary battle lands, ceasing all war. We can no sooner fall out of perfect standing with God than Jesus Himself.

The Gospel of Grace wildly proclaims an unbreakable Covenant between a Father and Son, with you standing irrevocably in Christ. No bad behavior can change it. No good behavior can improve it. Our role is simply whether we will *restfully believe* this too-good-to-be-true news.

When I first heard such an outlandish Grace—*it seemed dangerous.* Perhaps the reason such good news scares us is because we cannot begin to imagine how we would conduct our lives in a godly manner without the potential of punishment. *"If you tell them that, you'll give them permission to sin!"* Ironically, it is our belief of the truth that sets us free, not our fear of punishment.

In my old Christian life, there was nothing I wanted more than to be free. I had the desire but no ability. Coldplay sums up the way I felt, *"Oh no, I see. A spider web is tangled up with me."* The more I strove to rid my unwelcomed chains, the tighter they wrapped around my neck. Queue timely *Princess Bride* quote: *"Welcome to the Pit of Despair."* The crappy, Christian life marked by guilt and distance is torture-device level 50. It sucks. And sucks your life away. I tried my best and terribly failed. I felt the sting of guilt and wore the banner of shame—*damaged goods.* I grew only in fear towards God due to my constant and consistent not-measuring-up.

Fear always leads to anger. Anger, unchecked, creates hatred. I truly hated God. His knife on my neck didn't help. That fear-based religious expression eventually created in me a Tasmanian ganja-devil. If a spanking is the only thing keeping you in check, then you might be doing it wrong. I had little friendship with Love and had only known a taskmaster-motivator. *"Shape up, or I'll slit your throat."*

But... *Love.* Love is a superior motivator to fear. It doesn't scream, or grab, or threaten with punishment. There is not a controlling bone in Love's body. Love pursues. Love has no hierarchy, only family. Love doesn't emotionally distance to teach a lesson. Love draws close during a tantrum. Love compels. Love invites. Love supplies both the desire and ability for those invitations. Love intertwines with you. Love always speaks a better word than fear. Love doesn't even keep one record of wrongs. The eyes of Love see past the branches of your behavior and into the root of your beliefs.

36

It was, as I became convinced of Love and His washing words that my behavior and my surrender became Christ-like. Fruit on a tree is simply evidence of the planted seed. How many voices are calling for fruit without ever giving seed that bears it? If the correct seed is sown, that seed will do all the work of growing and bearing fruit. Grace-seeds in my heart did effortlessly what years of hard-slog striving never could.

Many of the Grace-seeds that set me free are in this book. *"Sin will not dominate you, for you are not under Law but under Grace"* (Rom. 6:14). The Law demands behavior change but doesn't lift a finger to help. It requires *your* self-effort. Grace supplies the desire *and* ability to do God's good pleasure by the power of the Holy Spirit. Our access into this Grace is by faith, and faith comes by *continually* hearing the words of Christ (Rom. 10:17). Notice that faith specifically comes from words concerning *Christ*. It is impossible for the Law to build your faith; it only gives birth to bondage. Much of the despair in my old-Christian-life was because the seeds sown, though godly in appearance, had no ability to produce freedom. When my heart became the soil for the person of Love, big-holy-fruits started growing.

I could choose the lifestyle of sin if I wanted, without *any* fear of punishment, and yet, I am compelled and supplied by His great love to walk as a King ought. The wells of His pleasure make flesh-indulging sin seem comical at best. What a cheap imitation of real satisfaction. I've feasted on good food and strong drink. Get that genetically modified corn outa-my-face! And what of surrender? I've built so much trust with Him. I've become convinced of His good nature. His touch is safe, and His leading is *always* for my good. His call to surrender is pure victory. When I surrender to Him, I don't have to surrender to anything else.

I thought not of behavior but of His fiery eyes, *and His love in me behaves quite well.* I thought not of surrender but of His goodness towards me, *and His love in me surrenders all that I am.*

PROMPTS

Compelled By Love

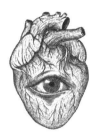

"For the love of Christ compels us, because we judge thus: that if One died for all, then all died" (2 Cor. 5:14).

Maybe you were compelled by fear for so long that it pushed you off the deep end like me. Take a few minutes, connect your heart to God, and ask Him to show you where He was and what He thought about you in your lowest moments.

Selah.

Now ponder your actions for God and for others. What is actually motivating you? Are you serving, helping, striving, doing lots of good things, but they are actually rooted in fear? To name a few: fear of rejection, fear of opinion, fear of failing, fear of missing out, fear of God's disapproval.

Fear robs you of love, which is why fear-based actions are *not* the golden ticket. Spankings can compel children to obey, but we are full-grown sons. Case-in-point: Have you experienced a guilt-offering at church? You know, where the speaker cakes on the pressure *so thick* that his pushy-disposition clangs over the Holy Spirit's whispering invitation.

Or maybe your own inward, guilty conscience has said this: *"If I don't put money in the plate, what will people think?"* Love invites. We respond with yes or no. Fear muddies the water of this beautiful, relational expression. Ask the Holy Spirit to help you identify your motivations.

Selah.

Invite the Holy Spirit into this moment. Fill your thoughts with the goodness of God and let His love wash over you and soothe your fears. Fears are just lies prodding your emotions. Ask Him to show you His thoughts toward you right now.

Selah.

SPACE FOR YOU

Catalog your dialogue.

LYRICS

Listen to: On Your Mind

Two o'clock in the morning inside
Simple life, I've been sipping all night
I was high as a kite in the summer of two thirteen

Deep down in my heart was shame
Didn't know You, didn't know where it came from
All the silent treatment that I felt

You were rude and hated from the page
Had a wrong view had a strong pain
I had gone and thought You were wrong for me
And even then

I was on Your mind
Before the world began
I was on Your mind
Even on my darkest day
You know even then
I was on Your mind

Nine o'clock in the morning on time
Busy life, I've been workin' all night
I was dry as a light in the summer of two sixteen

Deep down in my heart was stress
I didn't show it, but I didn't know how to hold it
All the burden bearing on my chest

We are one but I worked it on my own
Had a wrong view, had it alone
I had gone and thought you weren't there for me
And even then

I was on Your mind
Before the world began
I was on Your mind
Even on my darkest day
You know even then
I was on Your mind

Chapter Four

MADE FOR JESUS

Before anything was made—*The Father, The Son, and the Holy Spirit enjoyed ecstatic union.* Don't think of ethereal spirits snuggling. Think of a heavenly cabin in the woods where three distinct Persons are enjoying one another as One. It's weird. But it's God. From an overflow of eternal joy and benevolence: *"All things were made through [Jesus], and without Him, nothing was made that was made"* (John 1:3). Jesus created *all* the things.

He formed the seasons and fixed the time. He gave us smiles in the morning light. Creation flowed from pure love. It's comforting just to dwell on this: *the heart of life is good.* But have you ever stepped back and just asked, *"Why did He make everything? And, on the real, why did He make me?"* I've asked this too many times.

The recurring narrative I heard growing up was that we were created *primarily* to serve God. God was our Commander in Chief. The earth was at war. And we were enlisted in the Lord's army. *"Ask not what your country can do for you. Ask what you can do for your country."* Soldier-up young-buck is not Heaven's song. Myriads of angels were created to serve God, but we were *made for more.*

Receiving from God was frowned upon because that would have been *me-focused.* We'd think an earth-Dad is one strange bird if he told his boys: *"I made you to do things for me and give things to me."* This shamed-receiving mindset is kin to the Samaritan woman at the well rejecting Jesus' offer of living water: *"No, Jesus, I don't want to take Your living water. You need my water. That's how it works."*

Scene: Jesus has just finished loving a tree-hugging religious leader named Nicodemus in a town called Judea. His TripAdvisor had Galilee on the docket when a beautiful phrase appears: *"[Jesus] needed to go through Samaria"* (John 4:4). Why the detour? A woman on her sixth try at love.

This Samaritan lady filled her water bowl at the local well during the hottest part of the day to avoid the judgmental lips of her peers. There was a societal sense of shame surrounding both her heritage and her consistent divorce. She had divorced five husbands and was shacked up with a sixth, out of wedlock.

Jesus' motley crew went to the local market for bread, while Jesus struck up a conversation with our girl, *"Give Me a drink."* Jesus is setting her up to be free. She confuse-faced Jesus, *"For Jews have no dealings with Samaritans"* (John

4:9). Jesus quickly turns the conversation to focus on her receiving His water, saying, *"Whoever drinks of this water will thirst again, but whoever drinks of the water that I shall give him will never thirst"* (John 4:13-14). She might think Jesus is a gypsy, selling magic-well-water: *"Sir, give me this water, that I may not thirst, or come here to draw"* (John 4:15). Jesus then Jesus-jukes her with the prophetic and reads her life-mail. She at first perceives Jesus is a prophet, but eventually, her heart opens to see His real identity: *God in Flesh.* This divorce-ridden outcast has just been pursued by God on foot; fully seen in her mess, and still fully loved.

Our Samaritan girl tried love with six different men. The number six represents *man* as man was made on the sixth day. She had always tried to get her core needs met from men and only knew deep rejection. (It was unlawful for a woman to divorce her husband.) With each divorce notice, *the pain only deepened.* This perfect, seventh Man broke the pattern.

Jesus' posse returns and is offended that He is associating with a Samaritan and also concerned that their Rabbi is in deep, private conversation with a woman known for her man-swapping. They urge him to eat, and Jesus says, *"I have food to eat of which you do not know"* (John 4:32). Queue awkward side-eye disciple moment. *"Uh, did anyone give you bread, Jesus?"* Jesus' belly was filled by loving this rejected woman. When we give, we are depleted. When God gives, He is *strengthened.* Do you think Jesus would have been more delighted if He drank her water *or* she drank His water? This is our never-running-dry Jesus who loves to give and loves to love.

We tend to be the Samaritan woman looking for love in all the wrong places: *scraping, grabbing, and groping onto people in hopes that our inner life will be filled.* Just like her, we've returned to the same well, over and over again, but it keeps running dry. Invitation: drink from the well of eternal Life.

In the heart of the Trinity, before we were made, *Jesus was the beloved.* The Father perpetually poured His love out on the Son. The Son perpetually reciprocated in response to His Father's great love. It was from this holy union that Jesus' heart overflowed to the point of heavenly anguish—*Jesus desired a beloved.* Jesus loves to imitate His Father in mimic-like fashion. Jesus would show His newly fashioned beloved the same love His Father had shown Him. The Father watched in joyous celebration as His beloved Son created a world to hold his bride. And it was *very* good.

You were made, very specifically, to be the bride of a glorious Man. Things got pretty off-track from heart-eyes and garden-walking. We chose a rogue path and rejected the Fairest among ten thousand. There is no pain like unrequited love. Jesus felt the sting of our rejection from a Lover's eyes and to get us back: *He gave it all.*

Adam was formed from the dust, but Eve was carefully crafted from the rib of Adam. His bride was *inside* him, made *from* him, and made *for* him. Adam was delighted: *"Bone of my bone and flesh of my flesh."* This is a shadow. When the Roman Centurion pierced Jesus' rib on the Cross, the substance of this shadow came pouring out in blood and water. *You* came from Jesus' rib. *You* were in His heart before the foundation of the world. *You* were made *from* Jesus, and *for* Jesus.

You were the pearl of great price that Jesus sold everything for. You are His *dearly* beloved. He endured the great agony of the Cross for the joy of having you—*His bride.* A man who loves a woman will do crazy things for her. Jesus ventured through hell and back to wed you. He loved defeating death as it meant a forever-love with you. His *"Finished"* was great, big love. This is our valiant, ever-pursuing Kingly Husband. Jesus made you, gave Himself for you, is pursuing you, and is asking for your hand in Covenant-love. This stunning invitation is no killjoy. Jesus is Pleasure-King.

"You make known to me the path of life; You will fill me with joy in Your presence, with eternal pleasures at Your right hand" (Psalm 16:11). Read that again and answer this question: *"Who is sitting at God's right hand?"* Whoever this right-hand Man is has never-ending, ecstatic pleasures.

Hint: It's your Kingly Husband Jesus. What wonderful news it is that you were *made for Jesus.*

PROMPTS

He Put A Ring On It

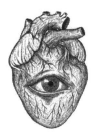

See Jesus getting down on one knee and asking for your hand in Covenant-love. Let this Man of faithfulness prove to you He is like *no* other man. Say yes to Him. Consent to be a bride.

Selah.

Your *Hubs* is a looker. He's like a diamond, and every which way you turn Him, there's a new shade of perfect beauty. The more we behold Him, the more we realize He is our true prize. Ask the Holy Spirit, *"Would you let my heart see the beauty of Jesus?"*

Selah.

If you have any questions about how a product was made or how it's properly used, you'll need the manufacturer's details. Jesus made you, and He's got the definitive blueprints for your make and model. You've been uniquely hand-crafted and masterfully woven together by your King-Husband in excruciating detail. Let the same hands that made you hold you. Sit and let your heart enjoy the affection of Jesus. This is what you were made for.

Selah.

What would you think if you saw a mother yelling at her baby: *"I'm hungry, baby! Give me food! Wahhh!"* Houston, we have a problem. *"You got it backwards, lady."* It is the mother's honor and joy to be her snuggle-bunnies' source. In the same way, your Husband *loves* when you take from Him. He is infinitely full of love, joy, peace, creativity, health, and every imaginable resource. If you could see, with the eyes of your heart, the wild generosity and inexhaustible supply of Jesus: *it would blow your lid.*

Ask the Holy Spirit to show you everything that He *desires* to give you. Receive *everything.*

Selah.

SPACE FOR YOU

Jesus vows.

LYRICS

Listen to: Made For Jesus

Deep in the caverns of Your heart
Stood Your beloved, Your daystar
The fairest among ten thousand wines

You formed the seasons and fixed the time
You gave me smiles in the morning light
Creation flowed from pure love

You were crafting
I was breathing
You were laughing
I was reaching out for You

I was made for heaven
I was made for Jesus
I was made to walk in the cool of the day with You

Cursed in the garden of paradise
You knew the pain from a Lover's eyes
To get us back, You gave it all
Filled in the likeness of flesh on earth

You bore the Cross that we deserved
You've gotten down on one knee

Spirit's breathing
Now I'm living
We've been married
Now I'm seeing
What I was made for

I was made for heaven
I was made for Jesus
I was made to walk in the cool of the day with You

The whole point of my existence
Is to know Your love

I was made for heaven
I was made for Jesus
I was made to walk in the cool of day with You

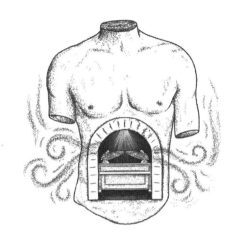

Chapter Five

CHRIST IS ONE WITH ME

In the previous chapter, Jesus offered the Samaritan woman His living water. In this dialogue, Jesus reveals a secret hidden for millennia, saying, *"The water that I shall give him will become **in him**, a fountain of water springing up into everlasting life."* Notice the location of eternal-life's fountain—inside of you! This is *the* mystery which has been hidden *"from ages and from generations, but now has been revealed to His saints... **Christ in you"*** (Col. 1:27).

Adam and Eve did not have Christ *in them*. This means God took their greatest failure and brilliantly found a way to leverage it to our eternal advantage. In the Old, God dwelled in a temple made by man, but in the New, *"Your body is the temple of the Holy Spirit who is in you"* (1 Cor. 6:19).

The temple in the Old, a shadow of you, had three parts: *The Holy of Holies, the inner courts, and the outer courts.* You, the new temple of God, have three parts: *spirit, soul, and body.* *"May your spirit, soul, and body be kept complete..."* (1 Thess. 5:23).

Your spirit is the *new* Holy of Holies. Your soul is the *new* inner courts. Your body is the *new* outer courts. Have you ever looked to the clouds and asked, *"God! Where are you?"* Well, you should have looked under your nose: *"He who is joined to the Lord is one spirit with Him"* (1 Cor. 6:17).

In the Old, God dwelled, very specifically, in the Holy of Holies, the innermost part of the temple. No human entry was allowed in this holy sanctuary minus the High Priest; AKA: one person on the planet. Although this was a great privilege, his access was limited to one day a year on the Day of Atonement known as Yom Kippur.

On this holy day, the priest would follow a meticulous ritual, enter the innermost parts of the temple, and sprinkle the blood of a *"lamb without blemish"* seven times atop the Ark of the Covenant. The lid that sealed the Ark was known as the Mercy Seat. This golden Seat was topped with two cherubim angels, protectors of God's holiness, who witnessed and decreed the blood's worth in the Courts of Heaven.

This day was most likely stress-inducing. Tradition speaks of a rope with bells being tied around the High Priest's waist in case of *death.* If even the most minute detail was missed by the priest, his birthday-suit would fail at the sheer magnitude of glory. His priest-friends, hoping not to hear bells on this day, held the rope outside.

We have a new Mercy Seat and no need for rope. *"And Jesus Himself is the propitiation for our sins"* (1 John 2:2).

Propitiation renders *"Mercy Seat."* Both the blood of the lamb and the Ark are shadows of Christ. In the Old, the blood of bulls and goats could *never* take away sins or make those who approach perfect, but Jesus offered Himself as *the* sacrifice for sins forever, making those who approach God perfect by His blood.

The Mercy Seat is a big-fancy-throne for a Judge. God, who happily sits on this golden mantle, cannot miss one microscopic speck of impurity with those glorious eyes. Our purity-infused Judge, in the presence of holy cherubim, continually evaluates Jesus' blood and will forever decree, moment by moment, in the Courtrooms of Heaven: *"Worthy is the blood of the Lamb!"*

Translation: Christ has made you so above-and-beyond perfect by His blood that He finds you a heavenly place to host His fullness. Your spirit, the modern-day Holy of Holies, has been fused as one with the Spirit of God: *"one spirit with the Lord."* This is what Hebrews calls, *"The spirits of righteous men made perfect"* (Heb. 12:23). Your spirit-man is vacuum-sealed, wall-to-wall Holy Ghost.

You, my friend, are the house of God and that reality is solely by Grace through faith. You cannot dare earn this spiritual new birth. *"Therefore, if anyone is in Christ, he is a new creation; old things have passed away; behold, all things have become new"* (2 Cor. 5:17). This word *new* renders: never before seen, completely unprecedented. Jesus has brought in the era of *New*.

While the Proverbs speak of the old heart as being deceitfully wicked, Prophets foretold of this new creation: *"I will give you a new heart and put a new spirit within you"* (Ezek. 36:26). I want you to pause and dwell on this: *you have a new heart and new righteous nature.* Your heart has been made new. Your spirit has been fused with Christ. You are a new creation having become a *"partaker of the Divine nature"* (2 Pet. 1:3).

When God looks at you, He doesn't pretend you're right with Him. He sees you as you actually are—*hidden in Christ.* You cannot afford to define yourself apart from your mystical, holy union with Jesus anymore. Ooey-gooey glad tidings. Christ *in* you. You *in* Christ. You cannot get on God's bad side if you *are* His side. He's the head. You're the body. You are eternally intertwined. You cannot afford to think even one thought about yourself that God does not think. And God sees, just as the Courts of Heaven, by the blood of His dear Son.

This new righteous nature is the reality that Paul always brought up to the question: *"Shall we sin that grace may abound?"* I'd like to point out he specifically says that where sin increases, grace does, in fact, hyper-abound. Case in point: Adam's sin led to Christ placing us on higher ground than we ever imagined. But Paul answers the question with a question, *"How can we, who died to sin, live in it any longer?"* (Rom. 6:2).

The sin in this verse is a noun—*the old sinful nature.* He puts the nail in the coffin, saying, *"We know that our old nature was nailed to the cross with Christ"* (Rom. 6:6). You might be stuck in your actions, or warped in your thinking, but it is not in your new righteous *nature* to sin. Your old nature and old heart *died* with Christ.

The Holy Spirit joins in this triumphant nature change via His New Covenant ministry. *"And when [the Holy Spirit] has come, He will convict the world of sin, and of righteousness, and of judgment"* (John 16:8). I always heard this verse explained strangely, which is unfortunate since Jesus gives the details in the following verse: *"Of sin because they do not believe in Me; of righteousness, because I go to My Father and you see Me no more; of judgment, because the ruler of this world is judged"* (John 16:9-10).

I want you to see this. The Holy Spirit is actively drawing those who *"do not believe in Me"* into believing in Christ. But the Holy Spirit is convincing the believer of his new, righteous *nature* in Christ. Why does the Holy Spirit do this? Jesus said, *"Because I go to My Father."* Again, Christ sat down at God's right hand *because* He had fully finished the work of preparing everything needed for the *new, righteous creation.* *"It is Finished!"* Jesus rose from the dead as the firstborn of this new-creation breed. The Head is birthed before the body. The Holy Spirit wants us to believe in our Christ-bought, new-creation nature. The belief of this truth will bear big, juicy fruit.

You don't have to dig very long into the soil of sex slavery to find this reality at work. Sweet, innocent, little girlies are brainwashed into thinking: *"I am dirty."* If you can deceive the mind, you can manipulate a will to bend to your liking. The belief of that one identity statement, *"I am dirty,"* can leave in its wake a lifetime of misery. And yet, we tend to believe something similar is true of our nature. Here is our rescuing Jesus, entering into our dirty-mindset and speaking, *"I see no spot or blemish in you, beloved."*

The verse finishes with the Holy Spirit convincing us of Satan's judgment at the Cross. The ruler of this world isn't the ruler anymore, and he ain't what he used to be. All the power that Satan had as *"ruler of the air"* was completely stripped at the Cross. The first Adam handed over his God-given authority to this outlaw. The second Adam, Christ, legally took it back. The only power Luci has now is borrowed via deceiving those with authority. We need to be convinced of this great victory. We are seated far above, and our warfare now is simply standing our ground in what Christ has done.

Where I used to believe the Holy Spirit was a dreadful nag, (confused for my guilty conscience), He *actually* believes in what Christ has done and desires to fully persuade sons of their true identity. As we believe these foundational Cross-truths, we will be set free. I say it like this: we *blossom gracefully into the full stature of Christ.* Side-note: the Holy Spirit still corrects and guides our path, but it's as righteous, new-creation sons.

As for our other two parts: soul and body. I do not yet fully understand this mystery but, *"We have the mind of Christ,"* and we are *"bone of His bone and flesh of His flesh."* This pairs nicely with, *"As Christ is, so we are in this world."* We are just all sorts of one with Jesus. May the Holy Spirit reveal more mysteries of our marriage-oneness with Christ.

We are a *new creation* people with access to incredible luxury; brided as one with God into an unprecedented, never-before-seen *new* creation: *Christ in us.* This is an absolutely incredible move by God. Nobody saw this coming. God has scooped us up from the garbage dump and seated us in heavenly places.

Truly, though sin increased, God's Grace super-abundantly hyper-abounded. The One who made us is now *one with us.* The River that springs up into eternal life is closer than your very breath! *Drink well, drink deep, and drink now: for Christ is one with me.*

PROMPTS

One With Christ

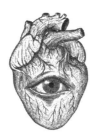

Life is closer than your very breath. Separation from God is a *lie*. You empower lies when you believe them; *believe the truth of oneness*. Turn your attention and affection towards Christ *in you*.

Selah.

Put your hands over your heart. Thank your heart for working so hard to keep you alive. Speak the same word to your heart that Christ speaks over you, *"I see no spot or blemish in you."* Bless your body with your words. Your body is holy and *is the temple*.

Selah.

You are not dirty, my sweets. Let the sweetness of the Holy Spirit wash over you. Ask Him to give you words to write down that define you.

Selah.

SPACE FOR YOU

The one with a pen ought to be one with Christ.

LYRICS

Listen to: Christ Is One With Me

Through shame from sin
Through rebel days
Through scar and barren land
Through darkest sea my anchor holds
For Christ is one with me

Through toil for soul
Through mission field
Through fire and stone from foe
Through shining sea my anchor holds
For Christ is one with me

Faithful
Faithful
Closer than a brother

Faithful
Faithful
Love beyond all other
For Christ is one with me

Through cross and nail
Through death and sting
Through grave and hades pyre
Through risen King my anchor holds
For Christ is one with me

You are
Faithful
Faithful
Closer than a brother
Faithful
Faithful
Love beyond all other
For Christ is one with me

You are one with me
Singing love secrets
You're singing love secrets
Over me

Chapter Six
ETERNAL VALENTINE

Valentine's Day can be the worst. When I was nerdy and alone, I lovingly referred to it as National Singles Awareness day. (PS: *Still nerdy.*) Another one of my favorites is, *"I'm dating Jesus this Valentine's Day."* Okay, Karen, we get it; you're single. I have embarrassing memories of whispering sweet-nothings as a 12-year-old squeaky-voiced boy pretending to be wildly romantic to my imaginary, super-lucky counterpart. Don't judge me. I'm not sure when, but somewhere along the way I became a hopeless romantic; the source of personal fulfillment *had* to be a rockstar relationship.

This wreaked havoc on my relationships. *"Your job is to make me happy and give me purpose"* is the mother of all expectations. I love how Danny Silk puts it in his must-read classic, Keep Your Love On: *"Powerless people approach relationships as consumers. They are always looking for other people who have resources of love, happiness, joy, and comfort to offer in a relationship to share with them because they don't have any."*

Consumers: it reminds me of being an introvert, where other humans, especially extroverts, are energy-sucking leeches. *"Get away from me, Teddy. I'm literally in the bathroom."*

I've had many relationships and friendships where I was the needy consumer. I didn't know how to create any of my core needs other than by consuming them from other people. In this unstable dependency, we imprison our fulfillment to the whims of another. Some of my relationships disguised themselves as healthy because my partner-in-crime enjoyed having a needy, dependent person in their life for the same reason—*to meet their core needs.* It feels good to the flesh to be needed. I was the consumer. They were the supplier. And there we were: *codependent and broken.*

The search warrant out for your core needs will always come back a bust if you're looking in the wrong place. No human, no religion, no calling, no ministry, no vision, no drug, no amount of money, no level of success, nothing under the sun can realistically or sustainably meet the needs of our soul. Deep cries out to eternal deep! I wonder how many moves we've made to a new job, a new relationship, a new addiction, a new-fill-in-the-blank, only to attach ourselves to another shallow well; rinse and repeat, dopamine-rush-of-newness in an eternal loop of looking.

There was a study with a billion-dollar budget conducted on this—*Ecclesiastes.* Solomon, the star of his own sad book, conducted an experiment to *"search out by wisdom all that is done under the sun"* (Eccl. 1:13). This is one man's lavish exploration into *every* pleasure the world has to offer.

Solomon was a rich playboy. The world was his oyster. When he built, he built *cities*. When he gardened, he planted *forests*. When he partied, he threw raves every night for *ten thousand* diehards. He employed the world's finest musicians to be his jesters. His mouth only tasted the *best* cuisine. He swam in the pools of romance, hand-selecting the most desirable women from *every* province. He is even to this day, inflation considered, the *richest* man to ever live. No one has even come close to the abundance of his material goods or experienced more worldly pleasures than our boy Solomon.

And his constant refrain? *"Vanity of vanities."* Solomon discovered a meaningless existence exploring the ends of the earth, and though God called His entire creation good, *none* of it substitutes walking in the cool of the day with the Soul-Maker, Pleasure-King.

There is a place in the garden of God where the ecstatic pleasure of Jesus satisfies each and every longing of our heart. *"Longing meets the shores of His delight."* It is from this garden that all of creation, which includes people, can be enjoyed in its beautiful and rightful place. If you've engaged Christianity and haven't spent much time in this luscious garden, perhaps you've been breaking your teeth on counterfeit-plastic-fruit. Or maybe you've just been flirting with your old hubby. *"Excuse you?"* Let's roleplay a bit here.

We've established by now that there are two covenants in the Bible: *the Old Covenant and the New Covenant.* These are marriage covenants with two different husbands. The husband of the Old Covenant—*Mr. Law.* The Husband of the

New Covenant—*Mr. Grace.* These two husbands treat their wives *very* differently.

Mr. Law *demands* perfection from his wife; nothing but flawless adherence to his commands will do. He cannot lift a finger to help. He has no fingers. He can only show, as in a mirror, his wife's ability to obey. He is, by nature, a cold tablet of stone.

Mr. Grace *supplies* perfection to His wife; He sees no spot or wrinkle in His lovely bride. Love compels Him to lay down His very life for His sweets. He is one with His bride and supplies all that she needs—*the desire and ability*—through His intertwined-ness with her. He can only show, as in a mirror, who His bride is through His grace-sparkling eyes. He is, by nature, a loving Husband. Not to mention, He is the fairest among ten thousand, a real looker—*the desire of all nations.*

In the everyday life of Mr. Law's bride, she strives day and night to please her husband! She gives *and* gives *and* gives only to see her husband, his arms folded, distantly demand of her. When she makes him breakfast, she knows that if the toast isn't *just* right—*he won't approve.*

"He really is perfect at everything he does," she thinks quietly to herself. *"And the things he demands are actually very good."* This bride has become quite skilled at downplaying her husband's ill-treatment. *"You know, it does seem like his full-time job is pointing out what's wrong with me, though,"* she dares to think.

This bride feels alone and is constantly anxious about her ability to perform. There's no music in the kitchen. And, those lights! They are unromantic, hospital lights. Longing for approval, she presents her best work before her husband. Mr. Law, with no heart capable of empathy, disregards her offering in unbending accordance with His perfect standards. The food was, in fact, not very good. To her defense, it is difficult to produce something wonderful in such an anxious environment.

In the everyday life of Mr. Grace's bride, she enjoys the richness of her Husband's love. They seriously need to get a room. She receives *and* receives *and* receives from her Husband, and He loves it. He never runs out of love to give. When she makes Him breakfast, she can barely focus on the toast—*His love-whispers romance her, and He is far more enjoyable than the meal.* He gently wraps Himself with her, holding and guiding her hands as she cooks.

This bride feels her Husband's full attention and never-altering affection. She forgets what anxiety is. He washes her with a waterfall of words. It is plainly obvious to this bride that her breakfast-making-skills have *nothing* to do with her Husband's acceptance of her. The music is soothing and sways to Mr. Grace's pulse. She presents her meal to her Husband, and honestly, she's not sure how, but it's the best food she's ever made! In such a loving relationship, her performance becomes effortless and wonderful. Mr. Grace enjoys toast. But He enjoys the nearness of His bride *much* more.

Wouldn't it be a pity if the burnt-toast-making bride that is married to Mr. Law never escaped her heavy covenant? *"By Law, a married woman is bound to her husband as long as he is alive, but if her husband dies, she is released from the Law that binds her to him"* (Rom. 7:2). If only her husband would die! That would free her. And yet, Mr. Law will never die. Not one dot or tittle.

Luckily for her, *"You also have become dead to the Law through the body of Christ, that you may be married to another"* (Rom. 7:4). What a glorious rescue by this love-King.

Mr. Grace even supplied the death that His bride needed to rid herself of a cold, heartless marriage.

Mr. Law is still alive. He still demands perfection from his ex-wives. Some of Mr. Law's angry-faced, pulpit-lawyers actually megaphone his demands to this day. Sometimes, the voice of Mr. Law is so loud she thinks she's still married to him. Sometimes, she confuses and mixes Mr. Law's spoiled wine with her new Husband's loving wine. There's even been days when she leaves Mr. Grace and returns to the harsh, task-mastering Mr. Law. You know, it can be very enticing to prove your worth. How Mr. Grace's heart rings with grief! He pursues, and like a summer rain cuts through the fog, *I have wiped out the handwriting of requirements of your old husband! I have nailed it to the very Cross!*" (Col. 2:14).

The bride whose heart is sure of Mr. Grace enjoys her marriage *so* much more. She's been convinced her old husband's demands have no legal precedence in her new marriage. For one, this bride has died, and the Law cannot demand from a dead man. Secondly, Christ legally fulfilled all the demands of Mr. Law in His bride's stead. Either way, the bride is free! This is one more free-ing reality of being *in Christ*. When He died, we died. When He rose, we rose. And we rose from death into a new marriage.

I lived in a strange three-way marriage most of my life. Two husbands with two different hearts mixed into one confusing Frankenstein-God. This marriage mixture is like Babylon—*the land of confusion*. Not much milk and honey in those lands. This is where many brides wander.

When I lived in Babylon, I thought God was schizophrenic. One minute He loved me. The next He loved deeply wounding me. On Sunday, *God loves you!*" Next

Sunday, *"He'll smite you dead if you take this bread and juice wrongly."* A husband that flip-flops between love and abuse is *not* a good one.

This back-and-forth religious whiplash produces some serious neck pain. The current version of God being heralded from a fleshly interpretation of the Scriptures is wounding the hearts of many, and often the rejection of Christianity is not the rejection of Christ. Religion infiltrated my view of God, and He became someone who was unhealthy, insecure, unsafe, and wildly conditional. Anyone in their right mind will run from marrying someone like that! It was shortly after I fully rejected my terrible-version-of God that Jesus showed Himself to me in the experiential power of the Holy Spirit as Love Himself. And I couldn't resist Mr. Grace. Many reject religious Christianity, very few, if any, reject the Pleasure-King-Jesus in all His loveliness.

Reality check: Sometimes, my emotions yell the opposite of what I know is true. Sometimes I find myself back at the whims of Mr. Law's voice and bear up under slavery of my own choosing. Sometimes I fall into old thinking patterns, place unreasonable expectations on people, and forfeit the joy of being Love to others. And that's when I desperately need the washing of His words of love to re-center me. It's then, more than ever, that we need to rest in Mr. Grace's garden, drink His wine, and let Him perfectly restore our soul to freedom. And He is very talented at that.

Result: Your relationships and friendships will become healthier and much more enjoyable. *"We love because He first loved us"* (1 John 4:19). Loved people love people. As you have freely received, freely give. The best receivers are the best givers; and the best lovers. Once the mother of all expectations, *"Complete me!"* is released, you'll be free to love like Jesus.

When you don't *need* a relationship to feel complete, you might be ready for a healthy one. While marriage is beautiful, holy, and good, this covenant is a shadow of a substance.

It is in this new marriage, this New Covenant, this ancient garden of Eden that we find those evasive core needs being met by sweet intimacy with Jesus. For your own sake, your family, and future, you can't afford to live any longer in such a dry and empty wilderness!

Whether you're feeling lonely in singleness or marriage, there's a new invitation for you: come eat and drink your fill in a Promised Land called completeness. This is where your inner world will find true satisfaction! This Land is an on-going exploration into your Husband, Mr. Grace, and it's in Him you'll discover you.

PROMPTS

Choose A Husband

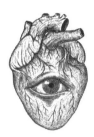

You have a gracious Husband that cares for you. He is pure safety. The greatest gift you can give to Him is your heart. Even if you're a hot mess, just open your heart to Him.

Selah.

Have you been confusing Mr. Grace with Mr. Law? Mr. Grace's treatment is like being washed under a warm waterfall. Ask the Holy Spirit to show you the ways Jesus has been wanting to express Himself as your loving Husband.

Selah.

After you engage with spiritual things, do you feel washed with Love? If you leave feeling worse than you did, you haven't engaged Mr. Grace. Ask the Holy Spirit to show you the voices of influence that you've allowed in your life that need to be silenced.

Selah.

SPACE FOR YOU

Mr. Grace enjoys toast. And letters.

LYRICS

Listen to: Eternal Valentine

Dreaming in the dust, now
Drinking in the sun, I'm
Soaking in the first morning of Your day
Enter the light
Stay for a while

How am I to hide
Eternal valentine, oh
How am I to love if not with You
Simply divine
Somewhere inside

Your love is a fire
Meets my desire
You are in the songs of my heart
Your love is a fire
You sing in my mire
Longing meets the shores of Your delight
And I, desire You

Divinely Intertwined, and
Drinking in Your wine, I'm
Feeling every pulse inside Your heart
Entered the bride
Stay all the time

Your love is a fire
Meets my desire
You are in the songs of my heart
Your love is a fire
You sing in my mire
Longing meets the shores of Your delight
And I, desire You

Chapter Seven
DAY BY DAY

I've had quite a few meltdowns about life. Have you ever looked to the sky and yelled: *"What is the purpose of it all?!"* Maybe I'm just dramatic. Whether stuck in a chair addicted to video games, pursuing higher education, toking the reefer as a prodigal, sojourning the States, or clocking the nine-to-five, I've always come to this internal crossroads of *"What am I doing?"*

Regardless of status, occupation, title, prestige, or locality: everyone has 24 hours in a day. Life is made up of moments. Moments turn into minutes, minutes to hours, hours to days, days to years, and years quickly become our entire lives. The small choices we make each day tend to determine everything about our life.

Instagram upon waking. Look at the ceiling for a few moments. Deep breath. *"Hey, Lord. It's Monday. Why did you invent those again?"* Step on all the unfolded laundry sprawled across the floor. Bzzzzz. That's my electric toothbrush.

Internal dialogue: *"Was that a dream about a unicorn?"* Bed-head mirror face-off. Attempt positive self-talk despite morning face. Jeans, boots, work shirt, watch, phone, wallet, keys. Surveying the landscape, *"I need to clean my room."*

"I believe in you. You're a success machine." (Plant-talk). Juice and bread. By His stripes, I am healed. *"Hi, Jesus. I love you."* Raw milk in a mason jar. Push pills. But healthy organic ones. Check the weather forecast. Daily: *"Too bad, I can't ride my bike all day."*

Ding. Third Floor. *"Hopefully, I don't have to small-talk in the elevator."* Vroom, vroom, my truck make big boom. 8:30 AM: *"Good morning"* (in a British accent). Work, work, work, work. 5:00 PM: *"Bye, fam."*

"Seriously? Learn to drive!" Grandma driver. Bless her, Lord Jesus. *"Hey, Siri. Start a bike activity on Strava and play Coldplay."* Fifteen miles on a good day. *"We live in a beautiful world. Yeah, we do, yeah we do."*

Tssssssssssssssssss. (That's what a sizzle sounds like?) Local food. Lots of seasonings. No recipes. Could be great. Or bad. *"I should probably practice music."* Record voice-memos with new ideas. Yawn. *"Wow, it's time for bed."* Zzzzz.

We all do things every day. *"Gee. Thanks, Captain Obvious. Great book."* Don't be sarcastic with me. I'm tall and can hide things on the top shelf if you are snarky with me. He-he. (I wonder if He-he has ever been in a book before.)

I've gotten lost in the mundane of life more times than I'd like to admit. If this routine business goes too long without soul-restoring enjoyment of Life Himself—*you might pop.* Or slow-fade into a general inner void of purpose-less-ness.

It reminds me of housekeeping. After a spring clean, you don't really notice the clutter after the first few days. *"It's just a few things out of place."* But neglect clean-as-you-go and your once minty-fresh becomes a disaster really quick. *"How? How did it get so dirty?"* One thing at a time. So it is with the soul of a man.

Scene: 2.5 million sun-kissed Jews just saw their bullying taskmasters swallowed by the sea. Their ancestors had spent 400 years being whipped and walloped by those cat-loving Egyptians. *"They made their lives bitter, forcing them to mix mortar and make bricks and do all the work in the fields. They were ruthless in all their demands"* (Exod. 1:14). Obey or get beaten. Hard-slog, hard-labor.

Free at last, free at last. Israel burst into song and dance-partied in the desert, praising God for deliverance from their harsh overseers. Fast-forward a bit, and these same praise-breaking once-captives were shoving God some serious profanities. *"If only we had died by the Lord's hand in Egypt! There we sat around pots of meat and ate all the food we wanted, but you have brought us out into the desert to starve this entire assembly to death"* (Exod. 16:3).

Nostalgia has a way of rose-coloring our past misery. These people wished they were still slaves. Then they wouldn't have to trust God for food. I think we forfeit our future sometimes for a more bondage-filled safety. There's some serious lack-of-trust going on in their speech: *"God, did you bring us here to die?"* I've thought that a couple of times when things looked sour.

God responded graciously to their murmuring. Sidenote: this is prior to the giving of the Law. Not one person died in Israel's entire Exodus journey until they asked for the Law. As soon as the Law was given, death erupted. *"The letter kills."* I believe God desired to relate to Israel based on the Covenant of Grace, which started with His promise to Abraham 400 years prior.

"Now to Abraham and his Seed were the promises made. He does not say, 'And to seeds' as of many, but as of one, 'And to your Seed', who is Christ" (Gal. 3:16). You can see here, the promise to Abraham *was* the New Covenant before Jesus put flesh on. God's heart, through Old and New, has always been grace and faith, however, Israel sidestepped their Father Abraham's faith-Covenant and basically said they would rather relate via merit. You don't have to trust God's goodness if it's based on you. I digress.

God's fresh grace to Israel's murmuring: *"I will rain down bread from heaven for you. The people are to go out each day and gather enough for that day"* (Exod. 16:4). I guess God isn't low carb. Heaven's bakery is probably legit. Somebody say amen. This free bread was *"like white coriander seed; and the taste of it was like wafers made with honey"* (Exod. 16:31).

These honey wafers from heaven were only good for one day. If big-eyed Jerry stuffed his pockets with more bread than he needed, the next morning, his wafers would be *"full of maggots and begin to smell"* (Exod. 16:20). This is an obvious exercise of daily trust in God's provision. There's grace *fresh*

for each day, and that's just how we're meant to live our lives—
day by day.

These honey wafers are still being made in Heaven, and a happy Baker is presenting them for our daily munching. While Israel had the shadow, we have the substance who is Christ: *"I am the bread of Life"* (John 6:35). Jesus said whoever eats of Him won't go hungry. Maybe that's where many of us have gone wrong: *we only collect manna every so often.*

We might even load up a truck-full of manna at big-epic bread conferences. Too bad it's rotten by the next day. As good as the cream-filled pastry was yesterday, you don't stay full by *having* eaten. Mountain top family-feasts are tasty, but they are not the daily special of our personal marriage with God. We have a glorious buffet available to us each and every day.

Be of good cheer if you've starved an incredible amount of days like me. *"I will restore to you the years that the swarming locust has eaten"* (Joel 2:25). Swarming locusts quickly consume big harvests. In one fell swoop, these devil-munchers can devour someone's entire livelihood. Has this happened to your *life?* This curse, along with every other, has been removed from the landscape of our lives by Christ on the Cross. We need not live in the barren wilderness any longer or submit to a very defeated enemy. The Promised Land is flowing with milk and honey, and it's yours, beloved, for the taking. God has given you a richly resourced land and wants to restore *all* your wasted time.

God loves restoring time. In fact, Jesus' first miracle was manipulating time. Our smiling Lord was attending a wedding party when His birthmother, Mary, said, *"They have no more wine."* Jesus proceeded to miraculously transform water sitting in six stone vats, around 180 gallons, into fermented grape juice. This heaven-drink must've had some nice legs because when Jesus' wine was served, the vineyard host complained, *"You're not supposed to save the best wine for last!"* Exquisite wine requires *decades of time* before a complex flavor-profile can form. It could've taken twenty years to generate the wine Jesus made and He made it from water in a few seconds. What may take men many years, Jesus can accomplish in an instant.

Jesus can compress time for you. He can restore all the days you've wasted or that have been stolen from you. He still loves turning water into wine. He's here now, and He's inviting you into a *new* normal. He desires to give you *"fullness of days"* where just one day with Him seems like a thousand years. Your old locust-days will be a faint memory.

Come to Jesus, your satiating carby-feast. Taste and see that He is good and watch Him turn all things for good. It is the daily eating of Jesus, our buttered bread, that will fill our bellies to the brim. I don't feel guilty when I don't eat every day. I feel hungry! Hey, you. Yeah, you. Get fat and happy.

PROMPTS

Mundane Magic and Spirit-Bombs

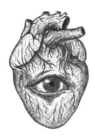

Have you been getting lost in *empty rhythms?* That's okay. The mundane can be magical with Jesus. Take a few moments, connect your heart to God, and enjoy His very nearness.

Selah.

Do you feel like big chunks of your life have been lost or stolen? When God restores, it's more than we lost and at better quality than the original. *"If a man steals a sheep, he must restore four sheep"* (Exod. 22:1). Jesus fulfilled this restoration-law for us at the Cross. We can believe for a great restoring. Ask the Holy Spirit what *He wants* to restore for you.

Selah.

Jesus said, *"Do this as often as you remember Me"* about Holy Communion—*bread and wine.* The wine represents Jesus' blood which was spilled for the removal of our sins. The bread represents Jesus' body, which was broken for our healing. When we take the Holy Communion, we *"proclaim the Lord's death"* because His death declares our victory.

There is an incredible amount of religious, restrictive teaching surrounding this sacrament. There is *nowhere in Scripture* that forbids the believer from taking Communion privately or often. You do *not* need another man, regardless of title, to partake Communion. The early church met in groups of twos to feast on Jesus in this way.

Get some bread and juice for your home. *You* are the priest of your home. Start *"proclaiming the Lord's death"* as often as you'd like. I like to do it every day. Communion is a bomb in the spirit. Evil spirits hate it because, at the Cross, their power was stripped. While you partake, *"fix your thoughts on the obedience of Christ [on the Cross]"* (2 Cor. 10:5). With the eyes of your heart, see the Great Exchange: your sin for His righteousness, your addiction for His freedom, your infirmity for His wholeness, your every need for His wonderful supply.

Selah.

SPACE FOR YOU

Write anything you'd like; perhaps, a restoration list.

LYRICS

Listen to: Day By Day

So kind is Your caressing
Drink You in like ancient wine
You've intertwined my being
Come hide away, day by day
You're always on my mind

You are in discovery
Wild and free
Charming Lover
Forever young
Shining Sun
Wading thunder
Fields of grain
Day by Day

Take me through Your seasons
Walk me in Your ancient grove
You've calmed my inhibitions
Come hide away, day by day
You're always in my breath

You were shaping the tide
You were making the lines
You were taking Your time on a bloodline
Just a lover in a garden and some flesh and bones
Soaking in the sun and the love that body groans
It was always You

You were loving the bride
You were ringing the chimes
You were looking like love in the garden aisle
Like some lovers in the summer
And some flesh and bones
Looking for that love that we lost
But we didn't know
That it was always You
It was always You

Chapter Eight
STRAWBERRY FIELDS

Have you ever been to a strawberry field? In the southern-charmed outskirts of Virginia, you can find a good ole fruit field every couple of miles. Pull your hitch on in the gravel lot, and hay-chewin' Roy (it had to be Roy) will fix you right up with a big-empty-basket for all your fruit-perusing needs. The best places let you, nay, encourage you to eat your fill while loading up. (I typed this with a thick, country accent.)

Hopefully, they've accounted this into their price per pound, because Mama didn't raise no fool; tell this six-foot-five white-boy he can have free, fresh strawberries and it's game-on, Wayne. I've thought about napping in the bushes for an all-day strawberry-eating fiasco, but that might be pushing the line. *Yeah, that's too much.*

When you pull a ripe strawberry off the vine, it makes a big popping noise. While the redness of fresh-picked is more vibrant than the truck- delivered store-boughts, it's the taste difference that will really throw your brain for a loop. How *wild* and wonderful that earth just grows these little sugar hearts of love. The first time I chomped into one, I went wide-eyed and copped an anger-face of delight. In music, we call that the *"stank face";* appropriate when the guitarist is slaying.

I can picture me now: *in general wonderment of a strawberry, blinking slowly in a random field.* I decided I had never *actually* tasted a strawberry before that moment. The supermarket versions are like eating shadows. There's something to be learned here: if I had never tasted the real thing, then I would've been content eating craptastic imitations for the rest of my life. The forever-lame empty shell of religion will never compare to the sweetness of real-Person, Holy-Spirit enjoyment. In this rare case, comparison is a great thing.

Why is supermarket fruit so much worse, in every way, than Roy's magical earth-candies? The modern fruit aisle doesn't actually have fresh produce and could be up to a year old before your pearly whites get to chomping. Chemicals, wax, and gases extend the life of our perfect-looking, dull-tasting American fruit.

There's a myriad of reasons our food isn't what it used to be. The soil is all wrong in big-business agriculture, which robs the nutrient density and flavor of our food. Monocultures instead of rich diversity. Droves of chemical spray. I'm not building a soapbox to reform the United States food industry, although it needs some major heaven-come-to-earth; the telling truth is that the real thing tastes much, much better.

Imagine getting used to God's fresh-and-juicy strawberries. You'd be so wine-and-dined on Goodness, the imitations the world has to offer would be hilariously dumb. *"Now that I've tasted the real thing, these factory-farmed versions are kin to turds."* I like to imagine Elf saying, *"You sit on a throne of lies!"* to imposter strawberries.

Public service announcement: while enjoyment of Him isn't a means for creating, every single thing I've ever made with substance is birthed from biting into a fresh strawberry naked and unashamed in the garden of God.

How To Eat: A Very Small Thesis

"How do I eat God's strawberries?" I feel a bit hesitant delving into this because *"No one will need a teacher to teach them how to know the Lord"* (Heb. 8:11). This word *know* is an experiential knowing that can only be described as covenant sexual intercourse. The Bible said it, not me. I think the point of this passage is this: you don't need or have to go *through* a man to know God anymore. You have direct access!

In the Old: the common Joe related to God through a priest. In the New: Jesus is our High Priest and He calls *every* believer a priest. If you feel dependent on a man, whether pastor or parent, to hear God's voice or have relationship with God, then you are in an outdated system of spiritual co-dependency that needs to be broken. *"Can you hear God for me?"*

Healthy New Covenant spiritual leaders try to work themselves out of a job by nourishing the priesthood and completeness of each believer in Christ. All leadership in the family of God ought to protect the autonomy and freedom of each person to know God personally. Paul was a great Overseer in this way: *"So-called believers came in by stealth to spy out our liberty which we have in Christ Jesus, that they might bring us into bondage"* (Gal. 2:4). In the context: back under Law.

Never let a man spiritually manipulate you with these words: *"You need me! And if you leave me, it's as good as leaving God."* Run from this man and run into Papa's open arms. Your covering is Christ; He's the head. You can taste, see, and intimately know God all for yourself. God moved heaven and hell for this wonderful invitation.

In the family of God, everyone shares equal access to God. No title, or accolade, or personal level of rule-keeping awards a brother or sister more access to God than the blood of Jesus. The Cross brings mountains low and valleys high. *"All shall know me from the least to the greatest"* (Heb. 8:11) crushes hierarchy and promotes a Camelot-style roundtable of equality.

At this table: older brothers and sisters don't just share fish they've caught—*they teach you how.* Is your family giving you a sip from their cistern or lighting the path to your own personal well? Do you feel like others are on the *inside* with God? They have *no* special access. Maybe they've eaten a few more strawberries. Hey: the dinner bell is ringing.

Practically, there are many ways we can taste, drink, enjoy, and know God. I'm going to share two that are the foundation of how I practice God's Presence. This is, obviously, not exhaustive.

First and foremost: *looking inward to Christ.* I've gone to great lengths to show, by the Scriptures, that *Christ lives within us.* I cannot, however, drink from His living water for you. By faith, you will need to press into the reality of your Christ-bought, Holy-Spirit-fused oneness.

Don't look to the outside for omens; the secret-sauce is not in the color of the moon or wet wool. While God used to live in temples made by human hands, now the fullness of God is pleased to dwell *within you.* In the Old: *men looked outward to find God.* In the New: *man houses His fullness.*

Turn your thoughts and affections towards the mystery of the ages: *Christ in you!* To experientially know this mystical, holy union of *in Christ* is the full-fat latte of true Christian expression. Paul's cry for us is *"to [experientially] know the love of Christ which passes [mere head] knowledge; that you may be filled with all the fullness of God"* (Eph. 3:19).

Christ is a real, living, breathing Person that lives within us. Practically speaking, I simply turn my affection inwardly toward Him, knowing I am His house. He is near! I don't have to fight for it. *"I don't feel anything, John Mark."* You don't have to feel anything. Emotions love to follow us. Simply turn your heart's affection toward Him and let your thoughts dwell on the richness of *Christ in you;* if for no other reason than *the Scriptures* testify of this reality.

Slap this religious non-sense of distance and separation in its ugly face. God is closer than the skin on your bones. He's fixed in you and isn't going anywhere. He has eternally planted His seed in you. This simple faith practice can be done anywhere, at any time, and is the real juicy goodness of love-relationship with God. You don't need a calendar reminder for this strawberry-tasting. You can enjoy Him all the time!

The second way: *Bible.* If you ask most Christians how to know God, the first response is *"Read the Bible."* And I agree with a caveat. God's written Word is a beautiful gift. I hope you've seen my affection for it. Let me say this: I spent so many years middle-fingering God, never reading the Bible, and basking in rebellion only to experience His unconditional love in a Wal-Mart parking lot.

In all my pre-Grace years as a Christian, one of my main battles was feeling condemned for not reading the Bible—*and sadly feeling condemned when I did read it, as I had no Spirit-Grace-goggles.* You read the Bible, *and* the Bible reads you. Condemned hearts translate condemnation from every passage; systematic or not.

I had been so beaten, battered, and bruised by religious teaching from the Bible that it PTSD'ed me at each page turn. I *desperately* needed a Teacher to teach me how to *rightly divide* the Word. One of the most practical keys is knowing the difference between the Old and New Covenants. Never let a teaching influence you if it doesn't clearly shine through the lens of the finished work of Jesus. The Cross splits history and changed everything. So many voices act as if Jesus changed *nothing*.

Quick epic overview: God *freely* gave the keys of earth to Adam. Adam effectively handed those keys over to sin and Satan. Jesus, the second Adam, legally took those keys back at the Cross and handed them to His bride. God has *freely* restored *everything* we lost and more. Colossians says it this way: "*[Jesus] disarmed all principalities and powers. He made a public spectacle of them triumphing over them by the Cross*" (Col 2:15).

This is our Savage-King breaking down the big-castle-door of death and victory-smashing everyone's faces in a thick pile of glory. To ignore Christ's finished work when translating or teaching any Scripture is to revel in ignorance. And we needlessly perish for a lack of knowledge! Our husband-King has won all authority, in both heaven and earth, and here we are *His adoring bride enjoying the spoils.* We can sign checks in His name and cash out all His resources. A wife's signature is as good as her husband's.

While Job longed for a mediator—*"Only if there were someone to mediate between us! Someone to bring us together!"*—we are *one* with God in a New Covenant with Christ as our Mediator Husband. Imagine reading Job, thinking nothing has changed. We've been placed in higher honor than we could ever imagine, sharing the right hand of God, in Christ, destined to reign and rule with Him.

Again: do not let teaching that ignores the Cross influence you. *"Beware that no one distracts you or intimidates you in their attempt to lead you away from Christ's fullness—for you are complete in Him!"* (Col. 2:8). Your wisdom, your faith, your righteousness, your love, your authority, your victory, your holiness, your everything comes from Jesus. He is our all-in-all. Let no one convince you otherwise! Christ *is* the sum of all things.

Scene: Two *sad-boy-disciples* are journeying home on foot. They're sulking over the recent death of their famous Rabbi. *"Those were the glory days."* Their Man had been deemed a heretic by the local church. *"What a gobby git; healing and feeding all those people."* The elder board, outraged, hired a hitman, *(the Romans),* to kill this menacing Jesus.

In the middle of our unnamed disciples' emo-conversation, *"Jesus started walking with them, but they were kept from recognizing Him"* (Luke 24:15-16). The force is strong with this One. Our risen, incognito Lord butts His way into their private conversation and asks, *"What are you talking about?"* They proceed to share their bad news, *"The chief priests and our rulers handed [Jesus] over to be sentenced to death and crucified Him"* (Luke 24:20).

It must be trippy hearing commentary on your own death. Jesus is stunned at their slowness to see and, *"Beginning with Moses and all the Prophets, He explained to them what was said in all the Scriptures concerning Himself."* Jesus' Bible study is unveiling Himself in the Bible. It is, after all, as we behold Him, we become like Him. Side-note: Notice that Jesus could have revealed Himself in person but chose to unveil Himself in the Scriptures first. At the end of their conversation, Jesus imparts the ability to do what He had just done, and *"He opened their minds so they could understand the Scriptures."* Jesus, Himself, must open our minds to see Him hidden in the Word.

This heart-veil was covering many in the first century, *"Even today when they read Moses' writings, their hearts are covered with that veil, and they do not understand"* (2 Cor. 3:15). This, unfortunately, could be the most accurate indictment on the modern-day church. Perhaps our powerless, untransformed lives are a result of ignorance in Christ's finished work. The Old is now a shadow of the substance— *Christ!* There are countless hidden gems waiting to be uncovered that unveil the beauty of Jesus. This process of seeing Jesus in the Word is the peas to our carrots. Here we are, toiling and striving when simply beholding Jesus will perform all the heavy lifting of our glorious transformation. Here's a great prayer: *"Open the eyes of my heart to really see."* This is not a killer-academic word-study. This is a spiritual heart-awakening to the person of Christ.

With Christ's victory in focus, reading God's Word is not a weight; it's an invitation to a feast. Sticking your nose in the Book is a great way to eat strawberries. While fleshly interpretations of these God-letters lead to death, the Holy Spirit will shepherd you into life-giving encounters with the Person of Jesus within the pages of the Bible. The chair is reserved for you, but there's no punishment for not coming to the table—*only hunger pains from missing the Great spread.*

If it doesn't smell like Jesus, then start digging, and ask your intertwined Love-King for eyes to see. He must be the one that opens your eyes to *really understand* the Scriptures. In all my excavating of passages that used to scare me, *a glorious Holy Spirit interpretation* has been waiting at the bottom and always leads to more life, more security, and more intimacy.

The strawberry-Creator prefers to be tasted more than studied. You could have a Ph.D. in Strawberries but know less than simpleton Roy who eats them. If the Holy Spirit were a country bumpkin, He'd be handing you a basket to fill. And along the path to God's strawberries, you'd see a big sign with bold letters: *"Eat your fill."*

PROMPTS

Chew Your Food

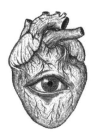

Let's get into God's Word and engage it in an experiential way. The written word is an arrow pointing to *The Living Word* in you. Open Psalm 23 and verse by verse: *dwell on it.*

"The Lord is my Shepherd and my best friend." Now take a moment, connect your heart to God, and start speaking this verse. Speak it until you feel it start to sink in. This is like *chewing the cud.* Dwell richly on it. Let your God-given imagination fill with Christ as your Shepherd. You want to get every last bit of nutrient out of this verse; let your heart marinate in the reality of it. Do this with each verse.

Selah.

SPACE FOR YOU

Strawberry-colored-ink could be neat.

LYRICS

Listen to: Strawberry Fields

It's like I'm running in
Strawberry fields with you
It's like I'm running in
Strawberry fields with you
Oh, taste and see
Oh, taste and see

Beautiful in all Your ways
Matchless in Your perfect peace
Open up my heart to taste
The wonders of Your endless grace

Chapter Nine
REST

Most of my gray-brain-matter was wasted on questioning my salvation growing up. I could not grow past this foundational question: *"Am I right with God?"* Without security, there is no intimacy. Without intimacy, there is no real knowledge. It's a bit funny to me, but mostly sad, looking back on some of my mindsets.

I was in my mom's basement and promised God in dramatic fashion: *"I promise I'll never sin again!"* afraid of a violent thunderstorm. I was convinced the storm was sent as a punishment from God to kill me.

After a long day of adolescence, I would kneel at my bed each night and confess every sin I could remember committing that day. If I didn't cover everything, I wouldn't have *"applied the blood"* and gone to hell due to my lack of correct confession.

I was lunch-conversing over some chicken-quesadillas with a few friends and used the Holy Spirit as the brunt of a joke. The look on their faces didn't bode well. I left convinced I had committed the unforgivable sin.

I self-sabotaged quite a few potential young-loves, sure that God wished me only to suffer by means of denying all sense of self; enjoyment was off-limits, and personality forbidden. To live this way was southern Holiness.

I muted the jokes that spontaneously combusted in my imagination. Stoicism was the most-holy trait of them all. God hated laughing.

These are just a *few* of the warped beliefs I held. Needless to say, when the Gospel of Grace ignited in my heart, at the age of 24, it was a good, strong drink. After drowning in sinking sand for so many years, the peace-inducing solid ground of Christ was too good to be true. To know Jesus as our righteousness is solid-rock foundational. This unshakeable security is the starting point for friendship with God; security begets intimacy.

Turns out, Jesus didn't *just* want to plant my feet on solid-ground, and then leave me to figure everything else out. He is endearingly concerned with our steps. I finally rested in Jesus as Savior, and on that foundation, *He became my Shepherd.*

> *"The Lord is my best friend and my Shepherd. [It's when I follow His leading that] I always have more than enough. He offers a resting place for me in His*

luxurious love. That's where He restores and revives my life" (Psalm 23:1, 2a, 3a).

Shepherds lead. Sheep follow. I would contend that the narrow path Jesus referred to is *following His leading in life.* How many know Christ as Savior but not as Shepherd? I was terrible at being independent my whole life, but I still boarded the struggle-bus of yoking up with Jesus. I had lots of practice making my own choices; no need to consult God. He wasn't interested in helping. And if He was, He would only lead me to boiling waters and poison pastures. Also, it's much more convenient making decisions on your own.

As I learned to be Shepherded, most of the time, I didn't really know how to discern His leading. This is the million-dollar question: *"Is that me or God?"* I noticed that rules, principles, and axioms are enticing to the flesh; they require less relationship, less giving up control. You can follow a principle without ever co-partnering with Jesus.

I was looking for a Person to lead me now. I thought He would speak paragraphs of words, but I've come to learn it's primarily through an *inward witness. "We serve not under [obedience to] the old code of written regulations, but [under obedience to the promptings] of the Spirit in newness [of life]"* (Rom. 7:6). Whereas we used to follow God by a code of regulations, now we have an intimate relationship with the Person and follow His inward promptings. This is a *new* way of living.

This witness of the Holy Spirit within us is a simple knowing. You've probably said, *"Deep down, I knew I shouldn't have dated him/her."* We all have access to this witness of the Holy Spirit, and I think it's this simple: is there peace or no peace? *"Let the peace of Christ rule your heart"*

(Col. 3:15). If you feel a pit in your stomach or can't kick an inward unrest: *wait*. Only make decisions when the promptings of the Spirit within you are yielding peace.

I know many wonderful fellow-Christians who trade their New Covenant inner witness for a lesser, outdated GPS: sensible logic, pro versus con, recurring numbers, the formation of clouds, license plates (basically turning everything into an outward omen), and the most common— *what other people say*. (You don't need a priest anymore, dude.)

Scene: A tear-ridden woman is recounting the woes of her dissolved marriage. Her counselor, in awe of the tale, asks, *"Why did you marry this man?"* Every red flag in the book made an appearance as the conversation unfolded. Her green light to join in marriage though: *"I saw a shooting star when I was praying and thought God was speaking to me!"* Turns out, the man she married was a shooting star—*here today and gone the next.*

Please hear me: I am not against outward messages of love from God. Outward signs, including prophetic words, are just not the *primary* way God leads His people and should only confirm what *Christ in you* is witnessing by way of peace. God is jealous of leading you in this way.

The life of the believer is *Christ in us*. It is this oneness, this indwelling of God within your temple, that being led by God makes sense. In fact, you and Jesus are so intertwined that I would bet you have followed Him on many occasions without giving Him the credit. Jesus has prompted me countless times, and all too quickly, I talk myself out of the invitation. Instead of eating from His Tree of Life, I pick from the Tree of Weighing Pros and Cons. Our Shepherd, who has only green pastures and restful waters along His path, knows exactly what we need, where we need to go, and when we need to move.

The question for us is always: *"Will you follow me?"* Which really translates: *"Do you trust Me?"* This is why being Shepherded is two-fold. Yoking up with Jesus in the outer world of our life-decisions is important. But how can we muster the trust to be led by another if our inner world is not flourishing? Meditate on Psalm 23, and you'll see a Shepherd leading us to the restoration of our soul—*the mind, will, and emotions.*

Have you ever heard the term *"Soul-winning"?* It's pretty inaccurate. Just like the Old Covenant temple, we're made up of three parts: spirit, soul, and body. Our spirit, which has been fused with Christ as a new creation, is as righteous, holy, healed, and whole as it'll ever be. We have identical DNA to God in our spirit-man. If the World-Breather Himself is within us *and* one with us, how can we house His fullness and remain in defeat? Our Christ-fused new-creation spirit lays perfectly dormant unless our soul aligns. Your old thought patterns need some major *rewiring* post-Holy-Spirit-fusion. This is why the tactic of the enemy is simply to deceive. If sons believe the lie, they live as slaves. Follow me for a few minutes as I paint this reality in fiction.

Rosaline Sparks: A Short Story

It was raining in London. Mr. Goldwin had just gotten off the phone with a world-class surgeon, and it didn't look good. Unphased by the news, Mr. Goldwin sunk into his father's ornate armchair and cracked open his favorite book. His golden-brown skin was covered in thick black hair. His eyes were kind and wore permanent smile lines.

The door creaked open, and Charley said, *"The mulberry trees are ready for harvest, Mr. Goldwin."* Charley, a sweet peach of a woman, often delivered this kind of news. She knew everything going on at the Goldwin Estate. She wasn't his wife or mother, but they were as close as two could get. Charley then said, *"Oh, and the pearl necklace. It's just finished. Rosaline will love it."*

One look at the mansion, and it was obvious Shepherd Goldwin was a wealthy man. His charming stone-castle sat in the middle of a richly diverse landscape—winding vineyards hugged every corner, thick walls of shrubbery fenced in cattle for miles, groves of fruit-trees scattered the grounds, raised beds housed every herb, flower-fields married plump vegetation, big pergolas shaded marble pools, walkways curved their way to hidden fountains, and a *thousand* more pleasantries. The upkeep required a huge host of hired hands. Every nook and cranny buzzed with chatter as the Estate's massive crew tended their various tasks.

Mr. Goldwin loved to pick mulberries. They were conveniently next-door to Rosaline's small wooden cabin on the east side of the Estate. Rosaline Sparks had been Mr. Goldwin's maidservant for ten years. Over the past year, though, her usual vibrant demeanor had been suffocated by an incurable heart condition. It was terminal, but her raw beauty still managed to shine through tired eyes.

After filling a bucket full of fresh berries, Mr. Goldwin made his daily stop at Rosaline's. Perched on the corner of her bed, he said, *"You're looking lovely as always, Miss Sparks."* Rosaline blushed. He was being kind, but she could tell he really meant it. He always seemed to have gracious eyes for her. *"I've got something special for you, Rosaline,"* Mr. Goldwin said. He then unveiled the majestic pearl necklace. *"Mr.*

Goldwin—I don't know what to say," Rosaline said in awe of the lavish gift.

"I wanted to celebrate the great news, Rosaline," Mr. Goldwin said with both tenderness and heaviness. *"They've found you a donor."* This was the news Rosaline never thought she'd hear. She responded in disbelief, *"Surely, they didn't find an exact match for me."* Mr. Goldwin replied, *"They have. Your surgery is in just three days."* Rosaline's eyes filled with tears of joy. She was to receive a brand-new heart.

Rosaline asked, *"Mr. Goldwin, will you make it to the surgery?"* Mr. Goldwin had been planning a trip to see his father for quite some time. From the stories Shepherd told, his father sounded like the most loving and happiest man in the world. Mr. Goldwin paused a long while and replied with a strange smirk, *"Yes. I'll be there."* His words were true but would transpire differently than Rosaline imagined.

The rain continued to fall in London when Rosaline underwent her heart surgery. It lasted six grueling hours. Her first visitor, Charley, peered through the hospital door and squeaked, *"Yoo-hoo."*

"Oh, Charley, it's so good to see you," Rosaline said with a smile. *"Have you come with Mr. Goldwin?"* Charley couldn't bear to tell her what had happened. *"It's just me, honey. But I've just talked to the doctors, and they said you've taken the heart perfectly. Good as new, they said."* The look in Charley's eyes communicated *something* was wrong. Rosaline's brand-new heart sunk, and she pried some more, *"Charley, what's happened?"*

Charley gathered herself, and said, *"Mr. Goldwin passed, honey. Last night."* Rosaline couldn't believe it. Mr. Goldwin had only treated her with the utmost honor for ten years. Everyone knew he fancied her. He asked, many times, for her hand in marriage and she deeply regretted passing on his invitations.

Rosaline's return to the Estate was met with emptiness. All the hired hands were nowhere to be found, which made for a peculiar silence across the grounds. *"Will you be alright, honey?"* Charley asked. Rosaline stared distantly over vacant Goldwin Estate and blankly replied, *"I can't believe he's gone, Charley."* Charley pulled close and sweetly consoled Rosaline. She was a great comforter. *"He was pure love, Rosaline,"* Charley said with honor. She then handed Rosaline a package covered in thick paper, *"He told me to give this to you after your surgery. He was adamant that you have it."* Rosaline accepted the gift and hugged Charley as if it would be their last. Charley, who could sense Rosaline's withdrawal, kindly said, *"I'll be by tomorrow to check on you, honey."*

Rosaline sulked in her cabin, put on her lovely pearls, and opened the strange gift. A dazzling picture frame housed a fancy-looking document and appeared to have Mr. Goldwin's signature. It was an odd gift seeing that she never learned to read. She, ignorant of what it was, center-pieced Mr. Goldwin's document above the mantle in her living room.

Twenty years passed. Goldwin Estate had seen better days. Mr. Goldwin was the glue that held everything together. Without him, it had become run-down and vacant. Rosaline was the last tenant left on the property. Her cabin, next to the mulberry trees, was falling apart. And, so was she. Rosaline, in her despair, went cold. Charley knocked on Rosaline's door year after year and was always met with silence. *"I'll try again tomorrow, honey."*

Rosaline often stood on the other side of her front door while Charley knocked. She had almost, many times, let her in. She had gotten used to rejecting the invitations of those who loved her. After twenty years of isolation, Rosaline finally resolved in her heart, *"I'll let Charley in tomorrow."*

Knock, knock, knock. Rosaline finally opened the door. Charley cracked the biggest smile you had ever seen and hugged Rosaline's neck. They nestled in the living room and enjoyed a lengthy, warm conversation. Famished from all the crying, their stomachs growled. Rosaline said, *"I'll make some soup. Make yourself at home, Charley."* Rosaline's cabin smelled like potatoes and cabbage. Knick-knacks sprawled the floor. Charley quickly noticed Mr. Goldwin's document housed above the mantle. She walked up to it and started reading its words for the first time. Her eyes widened as big as stones and she hollered to the kitchen, *"Rosaline, come here!"*

Mr. Goldwin's gift stood perfectly prized in that living room for twenty years before Charley took Rosaline by the arm, looked at her squarely, and said, *"Rosaline. My goodness. This is Mr. Goldwin's will. He's left you everything."*

Rosaline squinted in shock. *"Charley, no. That can't be right."* Charley began to read it aloud, *"I, Shepherd Goldwin, being of competent and sound mind, do hereby declare this to be my last will and testament... I hereby nominate and appoint Miss Rosaline Sparks as Executor..."* As Charley read each word, Rosaline's heart opened more and more. Charley paused on the last line of the document. *"Oh, my word, honey."* Rosaline asked, *"What is it, Charley? What does it say?"* Charley whispered, *"He was your donor."* Mr. Goldwin had willingly given his life for his love, and in his death, left all that he had for her.

Rosaline needlessly lived as a maidservant for *many* years. Although her Master *freely* gave everything to her, she didn't lay claim of the great spoils due her lack of knowledge. Her inheritance, lavish and potent, hid right under her nose in perfectly plain sight. While she could have moved into the palace, she remained in poverty. It is also of great importance to realize: if she heard the glad tidings of her glorious inheritance and *not* believed the report, still it would have benefited her nothing. So it is with many of us.

We have been afforded all things and have remained unaware for far too long. Christ, the source of all things, has given us all of Himself and all of His resources. *"Be transformed by the renewing of your mind"* is like turning a valve. Unaware of who we are and what we've been given, we lock Christ away in the cellar of our spirit. Our framed inheritance has been collecting dust on the wall. It is when the mind is renewed that our spirit-doors swing wide and all the goodies of Christ come flooding through. *"Be lifted up, you everlasting doors! And the King of glory shall come in"* (Psalm 24:7).

We have *all* of Christ. His nature, His love, His wisdom, His kindness, His honor, His healing, His power, His everything has *already been deposited in* us. We've already got it. As we renew our mind to this rest-filled finished-ness, the valve opens, and Christ fumigates our temple like the *altar of incense*. This is our soul *"being filled with the fullness of God"* (Eph. 3:19). You could say it this way: Faith receives by acknowledging what Grace has already given. *"Your participation in the faith becomes effective by the acknowledgment of every good thing which is in you in Christ Jesus"* (Philemon 1:6).

No wonder our dear Shepherd longs to restore the inner world of our soul. Our beloved John wished above all things that *"your soul prospers"* (3 John 1:2). To the extent that our mind is renewed to Christ, is the extent we'll see heaven rushing out from our spirit-man to cover the ends of the earth. Renew the mind, release the Spirit.

Practically speaking: our mind, our will, and emotions need an alignment with Christ. *"Take your thoughts captive to the obedience of Christ"* is your thought-life fixed on Christ's finished work. Your emotional world and temperament, a gift from God, will prosper as your mind stays fixed on Christ. Your will, (which is what you desire), is morphed and molded by beholding Christ, the innate desire of all nations. *"Delight yourself in the Lord, and He will give you the desires of your heart"* (Psalm 37:4).

When Jesus is the Shepherd of our soul, we lack absolutely nothing. If we allowed ourselves this luxury of being restored by Jesus, our inner world could be so healthy that, even in the darkest valley, we won't entertain fear. *"Even when I walk through the valley of death's shadow, I will not fear."* Love is great soil for the soul. This Shepherd is so confident in His love bringing strength to our soul that, *"He sets a table for me in the presence of my enemies."* This is like chowing down on the grub of peace while those who oppose you breathe right down your neck.

A restored soul aligned with Christ—*who He is, what He says, what He's done*—is a cup *overflowing*. His fullness, within us, will spill into every area of our outer world; *decisions included*. Jesus, the Restorer of souls, is asking, *"Are you tired and worn out? Come to me, and I will give you a real rest."*

PROMPTS

Shepherd Of The Soul

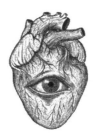

When a dog has been beaten by the hand of its old master, *you can tell.* Even if your intentions are pure gold, when you lift your hand to pet an abused pooch, his eyes will wince. He's unsure if your hand is meant to harm or to hold. Those fear-triggers are particularly strong if you resemble the abuser.

Ask the Holy Spirit to help you identify the parts of your heart that do not yet fully trust in the overwhelming goodness of God. Let Him reveal the points where you got stuck and started believing the great lie: *God is not good.*

Selah.

Invite the Holy Spirit to replace these warped pictures of God with new ones. To help stir your imagination, read 1 Corinthians 13:4-13. Take each line slowly. Take a moment, connect your heart to God, and let the words sink in.

Selah.

After you've rested your inner man in His luxurious love, bring forward a decision you've been weighing. As you bring this decision to the forefront of your heart: do you sense an inward check, or do you feel a calming, increase of peace?

Selah.

Water filters are crucial in this day and age; the high-quality ones absorb countless heavy metals, acids, and chemicals. In similar fashion, our thought life needs some quality filtering. Do you filter every thought *through* the finished work of Christ on the Cross? The state of your emotional world is a great litmus test; it showcases what your mind has been fixed on. Ask the Holy Spirit to filter your thoughts through Christ's work on the Cross.

Selah.

SPACE FOR YOU

Perhaps, an attempt at coining Jesus' will.

LYRICS

Listen to: Rest

If you wanna see the Kingdom
Become like a little child
If you wanna see the Kingdom
Become like a little child, and

Rest
Rest, oh yes
Rest
Rest, oh yes

Working, running, spinning
Busy, busy, busy
He makes you lie down and rest

Chapter Ten
ABBA

Have you ever thought about who you feel most connected to—*Jesus, the Father, or the Holy Spirit?* I was asked this for the first time during a healing prayer; *(it's like Holy Spirit guided counseling)*. My immediate response was *"Pops."* This was not always the case. My view of Father God teetered the line of abusive Rager drunk with pride. I fueled my dislike for the Divine with various jaded practices, *none-more-fulfilling* than Bible-mocking blogs which pull out the verses we sweep under the rug; *i.e., children-death via bears.* When I *encountered* God as a tender-hearted Father in my beet-red 1993 Honda Accord, I was shaken, to say the least. I tell people that it wasn't until then, in that Father-son moment, I entered manhood at the age of 24.

It was no coincidence that at the awkward crux of puberty, I hid behind a computer screen for five years. I was afraid of the responsibility of manhood and did what boys do: *hide*. Prolong that adolescence into college, and I found a glass bong to hide behind. I responded to life with fear—*the fear of failure, the fear of responsibility, and a deep-seated inadequacy*. I could not lead myself and, god-forbid, a family. Fear drives some people into anxiety-action. It pinned me down into debilitating passivity. When I packed my bags to leave college, I felt like a boy in a man's world: *un-equipped to tackle life*.

I'm not sure if there's anything troubling our world more than the effects of fatherlessness. Regardless if a father is physically absent, emotionally unavailable, or actively unhealthy, every child is imprinted with the same core-needs: *a Father's affirmation, approval, and acceptance*.

Read any study on the effects of absentee-fathers, and you'll see a mountainous increase of aggression, depression, addiction, low self-esteem, drug abuse, jail time, and suicide. I think it's safe to say we need a heavy dose of Fatherly affection. Beautifully, the centerpiece of God's heart is to become *"Father to the fatherless."* And, yet, in a religious landscape addicted to performance, very little, if any, of the Father is revealed. Jesus was King at disrupting religious mindsets about God and came to reveal one name: *Father*.

Scene: Some prostitutes, a few degenerates, and some dirty reps from the IRS are hanging out with Jesus. The local pastors, squinty-eyed and bougie-faced, mutter, *"This man welcomes sinners and eats with them."* Picture Malfoy from Harry Potter. Every small-town gossip-lover knew the history of these outcasts, and it stirred the pot *real* good. Maybe the harlots mentioned were some ex-wives of the closet-lusting pastors. These community-branded sinners committed various heinous crimes and were punished with ex-communication. And tax-collectors? They wore shame as their banner most likely afraid of who they had become—*ex-Jews who betrayed their own people to work for Rome and collect hefty taxes.* This is your brother getting rich from your audit.

Religious leaders drowned this crowd in judgment to the point that they wouldn't ever deal directly with them. Rabbis audibly listed these scumbags at church on Saturday so everyone could join in the shame-fest. *"Make sure you spit in their face and take a bath if you get near them."* These were the unclean untouchables.

And here's Jesus: sharing a meal with them, having a jolly good time. Big-laughs and knee-slaps. To dine together in this culture was something like a covenant. You carefully selected who to break bread with as it was saying, *"I will share your status in society."* Jesus' meal-sharing said, *"I will accept the shame that everyone shames you with."* It's no wonder Jesus was famously known as the *"Friend of Sinners"* as He intentionally stood in solidarity with the local rejects. God loves the most unclean, untouchable people. He reaches into our deepest shame and stands in it with us. This is a hard pill to swallow in a self-righteous work-for-it religious system.

Jesus puts down His wine and responds to the religious griping with three parables: the lost sheep, the lost coin, and the lost son. A good Shepherd, Jesus, leaves the ninety-nine to find the one. A woman, the Holy Spirit, leaves her nine coins to draw the one who is lost. Finally, a Father enters into His son's shame with love. When Jesus tells the story of the prodigal son, it is specifically to reveal the heart of God as Father.

Get your tissues. This story is a tear-jerker. *"A certain man had two sons. The younger one said to his father, 'Father, give me my share of the estate'"* (Luke 15:11). Inheritance didn't officially transfer until the father's death, which means this son has just passive-aggressively said, *"I wish you were dead."* This little tyke takes his daddy's Benjamins and sets off for *"far country,"* which is Hebraic language for forsaking covenant and yoking with the ungodly.

He basically hit up Vegas and blew his inheritance on hookers and the slots. Famine hits and pushes him further down, leaving our lost-boy as a grunt-worker at a pig-poo-encrusted factory-farm. He is so destitute that he *"longed to fill his stomach with the pods that the pigs were eating,"* but no one would even let him eat their genetically modified slosh.

Mind you, Jesus is telling this story to Jews who viewed pigs as an unkosher abomination. Each word probably gag-refluxed these pastors; this reprobate is rolling in the mud with a Gentile pig-farmer. You could imagine the hatred beginning to boil for even mentioning this unspeakable crass.

Our destitute poo-boy *"comes to his senses"* and thinks, *"How many of my father's hired servants have food to spare, and here I am starving to death!"* (Luke 15:17). Please notice the lack of heartfelt motive. This son shows no grief of disowning his father. He's starving and trying to fill his belly. This is *not* repentance. This is self-interest. Hungry, he starts his trek home with a canned speech: *"I am no longer worthy to be called your son; make me one of your hired servants."*

Meanwhile, the father of this prodigal son has been scanning the horizon each night in hopes of his return. His neighbors pity him, *"Poor old man is still looking for his son."* They also think him weak and *without honor* for not disowning his *dishonoring* son. And then it finally happened one night: *"But while he was still a long way off, his father saw him and was filled with compassion for him; he ran to his son, threw his arms around him and kissed him"* (Luke 15:20).

The father has just shamed himself to the surrounding community. It was dishonorable for older men to run and even more so to pick up their robes for an all-out sprint. There was not an ounce of hardness in the father's heart towards His son— *only compassion*. He ran and *"fell on his son's neck"* with many kisses, despite the gagging smell of pig feces. This father forsook his reputation, said *to hell* with what other people thought of him, and embraced his rebellious son.

Before the son could finish his canned speech, the father said, *"Quick! Bring the best robe and put it on him. Put a ring on his finger and sandals on his feet. Bring the fatted calf and kill it. Let's have a feast and celebrate"* (Luke 15:22-23). The son planned to *"become a hired servant,"* but his father would have nothing of the sort.

The Father's best robe communicated, *"you are still my son"* despite the betrayal and feces. A ring in this day was like a credit card. Immediately restoring the family signet and sandals, he said, *"All that I have is still yours. You don't have to work for it."* Where the son might have expected shame, the father threw a feast.

My friend, you might have run to *"far country,"* but the Father is waiting on His front porch, ready to run towards you and *kiss* you. Stop trying to wash your clothes of the mess you've made. Your Father will give you His *best* robe to wear. When He sees you, His heart is moved with compassion. *This* is your Father!

Maybe you've been planning to work your way back into His good favor. He'll have nothing of it. The Father wears Grace as His banner. His kitchen is always roasting a fatted lamb ready for your return. There is no one as lavish and joyful as our Father. He loves you and keeps no record of your shaming Him. His love covers a multitude of sins. He will *sing and dance* at your return. He invites you to feast as a full-fledged son!

The story continues: *"Meanwhile, the older son was in the field and heard music and dancing."* This older brother, who is confused by joy, asks, *"What is the meaning of this?"* and is stunned to find out this party is for his degenerate brother. *"The older brother became angry and refused to go in"* (Luke 15:28).

The father pleads with his elder son but is met with anger: *"Look! All these years I've been slaving for you and never disobeyed your orders! Yet you never gave me even a young goat!"* This older brother would prefer his service and performance to be the standard for acceptance and blessing. To which the father replies: *"My son, you are always with me, and everything I have is yours"* (Luke 15:31). Whether prodigal or goody-two-shoe, the Father's invitation is always the same: Grace. *"Everything that I have is yours. You need not work for it."*

We have the best Dad in the whole world. Is that foreign to you? Maybe you're living in a long line of father-brokenness—*fathers repeating the sins of their fathers and their fathers before them.* This is what the more spiritual people call generational curses. Luckily for you and me, this pattern can break now: *"Christ became a curse for us. For it is written: 'everyone who hangs on a tree is cursed.'"*

Believe with me now that you are the start of something *new*. Your heavenly Father has made every provision for you to be completely free from every curse. Settle it in your heart now: *in Christ* is the power to break every pattern of dysfunction in your family line. *"It stops with me."*

For men: Manhood is a gift we receive from our Father. No crucible can earn it; no axiom can bring it. We are ushered from boyhood to manhood, from cursing to blessing, by the words of our Father: *"You are my beloved son. I love you, son. I am so pleased you are My son. All that I have is yours."*

Consent to the love of the Father. Start calling Him, *"Dad!"* Start calling Him *"Abba!"*

PROMPTS

The Father Breaks Chains

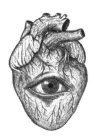

Take a moment, connect your heart to God, and dwell on the Lord as your kind-hearted Dad.

Selah.

Every day is a great day to break the chains that have held you down. The enemies you've been facing have already been defeated, and every curse is already broken. Christ's death *is your victory*. Come into alignment with this anchoring reality. Your *agreement* of the truth opens the door to its power. *"What you loose on the earth, will be loosed in heaven"* (Matt. 16:19).

Maybe you've believed the lie that you *have no victory*. My friend, you've been opening the door to death by agreeing with the lie. Repent in Greek is *metanoia*. *Meta* means change. *Noia* means mind. Renew your mind to the truth of your victory *in Christ* over every curse. This is where the rubber meets the road in our transformation. Believe the truth, and let it set you free. In Christ, *you are* free from every curse. Let the eyes of your heart see Jesus on the Cross redeeming you from every sin, every addiction, and every curse.

Selah.

Hear the Father speaking these words over you: *"My son. Oh, how I love you. I am so pleased with you. I am so proud of you. You are My delight and My joy. Here are My best robes. Here is My ring. Everything I have is yours."*

Selah.

Call God, *"Dad."* Start talking to Him like a healthy one.

Selah

SPACE FOR YOU

Write it down, child.

LYRICS

Listen to: Abba

I never solve all the formulas I've created
I know Your heart is more than
Just a law to pay the bills
I want to walk inside the cool of the day
With simple affections of Your heart
I wanted everything in nine to five and Devo time
Sometimes I make life a simple cell

All I need and
All I want
All I care for is

Abba, all I know is Abba
Abba, all I know is
Abba, I belong to You

I never long to be satisfied when communing
I know Your love is all the drink I'll ever need
I want to walk inside the cool of the day
With simple affections of Your heart
I'm found in everything You did for me

And nothing more
Sometimes I make life a simple song

All I need and
All I want
All I care for is

Abba, all I know is Abba
Abba, all I know is
Abba, I belong to You

You are
Singing and dancing
Over your sons
Smiling and beaming
Your Father's love

Chapter Eleven

I DON'T KNOW ANYTHING

Pride comes before a fall. I still remember defending religious half-truths to my swirly friends when I was a confused, bound boy; anything I hadn't been indoctrinated with—*it offended me.* Emotions would flare, and ultimately a dividing line was made. The *focus* of conversation was on doctrine. *"I need to pin down exactly what you believe so I can categorize you and see if you have perfect theology like me."*

This is not uncommon. Similar divisions were happening amidst different *religious* factions during Jesus' day. The Pharisees, Sadducees, Essenes, and Zealots were the denominations at odds on various doctrines in Jesus' Jerusalem; politics, end-times, interpretation of Scriptures were the main topics up for debate. If you follow Jesus' story in the Gospels, you'll actually notice these factions attempting to trap Jesus with theological questions; whether in hopes he would agree for their pride's sake or disagree for His prosecution, I'm unsure.

As a little sponge growing up in western Christianity, one of the most confusing bits about the whole deal was how many contrasting voices there were. If ancient Jerusalem had four, modern-day has thousands. I anger-face-palmed a few too many times at the overwhelming noise of opinionated Churchianity. My brain felt like primordial soup in the cauldron of religious jargon.

This melting pot of doctrine always reminded me of *The Paradox of Choice*. This paradox says that we love our freedom to choose, but with too many options to pick from, this freedom becomes an anxiety-inducing weight. We do this at restaurants with big menus. *"What's your best dish?"* This is basically saying you have too many choices, and you would prefer less to make an informed decision.

More isn't always better—*a mantra adopted by some of the most successful companies in the world.* For instance, Apple's branding, marketing, and options are simple; whereas you're likely to get lost in the abyss of choice somewhere else. The theory is, with the perfect amount of *fewer* options, you feel better about your decision, which makes for a thicker dopamine hit.

As the world gets smaller, our option-diversity ten-folds for everything: who to marry, which career to pursue, where to live, what vehicle to drive, what kind of house to buy—*you name it.* Perhaps one reason we're all getting married later in life is because we just can't make up our minds with *so* many options.

Do you feel this way about belief-systems? I kind of do. And while I do believe that knowing what you believe and why is important, it's ultimately not the secret sauce. I don't think we should huddle around a doctrine, or teaching, or personality. Jesus said to the forever-debating-pastors of His day that they had been searching the Scriptures for life when Life Himself was standing before them.

Imagine if the four AWANA-clubs of Jesus' day simply drew close to Jesus. Regardless of their peripheral beliefs, I know He would have made no distinction and gladly received them. Sometimes we can honor our belief of the truth in word but not honor the heart of Jesus. *"You honor me with your words, but your hearts are so far from Me"* (Matt. 15:8).

Jesus is the fire we should cozy around. My hope for you and for me is that, amidst our peripheral disagreements, we can find our common ground, which is in the *person* of Jesus. And when we do disagree, we do it with utmost honor knowing that we are equal heirs as sons of God. Big-fat-eye-logs removed.

If I'm honest about my journey-of-belief: the peripherals have been in a constant state of metamorphosis. This is another way of saying: I'm open to correction, and I could be wrong. You're powerful to agree or disagree. Let's tear up our annual pass to the local conformity club and wear brotherly love. If my systematics are on point, but I have not let my Kingly Husband kiss me on the lips, then I've made a silly trade.

One thing I do know: I am growing in relationship with the person of Jesus, and His heart is always becoming more gold to me. Christ, the Person, is pure majesty and wonder. He's often removed scales from my eyes to which I can only respond: *"I don't know anything about anything anymore."* One thing I do know: I know Him more than I did yesterday. I just want to continue discovering His heart-treasures and that journey will take a pretty long time. I think *eternity* is a good place to start.

PROMPTS

The Door Is In The Floor

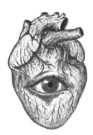

Ask the Holy Spirit to remove the need to be perfect. Sit a moment in the reality that you don't know everything. Let the mystery of Christ in you overwhelm your need to be right.

Selah.

SPACE FOR YOU

If you know everything, there's nothing to explore.

LYRICS

Listen to: I Don't Know Anything

Open my heart
Expand, expand
Open all I am

I don't know anything about anything anymore
All I know is You more than I did before
Your heart is always becoming more gold to me

I don't know anything about anything anymore
Except I know You more than I did before, Lord
I wanna know all of the treasures in Your heart
I'm sure eternity's a good place to start

Open my heart
Open all I am

Chapter Twelve
DIAMONDS AS YOUR SKIN

"Immediately, I was in the Spirit; and behold, a throne set in heaven, and One sat on the throne. And He who sat there was like a jasper and a sardius stone in appearance; and there was a rainbow around the throne, in appearance like an emerald. Around the throne were twenty-four thrones, and on them, I saw twenty-four elders sitting, clothed in white robes; and they had crowns of gold on their heads. And from the throne proceeded lightnings, thunderings, and voices. Seven lamps of fire were burning before the throne, which are the seven Spirits of God." (Rev. 4:2-5).

Let's get mystical, mystical. Let's get mystical, mystical. (I hope you get this musical reference.) Our beloved John is *"in the Spirit"* seeing heaven. He sees God on the throne with an appearance of precious gems. Around our diamond-cut Lord is an emerald rainbow, twenty-four golden-crowned elders in white robes with their own mini-thrones, talking-storms(?), and seven burning lamps which John decisively says are the *"seven Spirits of God."*

If you read the Bible, you can find some serious whack. This is a non-extensive list: death via body-turning-to-salt, talking donkeys, rods transfiguring into snakes, seas opening into walkways, bread falling from the sky, magical-ever-increasing-oil for widows, fire-tunnels, furnace-proof men, dead-raising, transportation via fire chariot, bookoos of angelic beings intimately involved in world affairs, gravity-defiance, heaven-visitations by living men, all kinds of physical healings, flying, water-walking, poison-immunity, teleportation, and a lot more.

Countless saints of old have recounted mystical experiences with God from kind-of-cool all the way to they-might-be-cray. I listened to a podcast as a man recounted his heavenly encounter with God. *"His skin was diamond and oil ran down His chest."* He spoke as if he experienced heaven. He didn't die. He just went.

His main point was the door to heaven is not death. It's Jesus. And since we have Him now, we can, with the eyes of our heart, visit anytime we'd like without waiting for the Grim Reaper. I mean, it makes sense. I'm a pretty down-to-earth person, but if the reality that we are seated in heavenly places with Christ is something *that* experiential, *then I would be down.* Speaking of death, this reminds me of: *"Everyone wants to go to heaven, but nobody wants to die."* We've already died with Christ and risen to *new* life. If our body stops working, we just shed the birthday suit—*we don't die.* Maybe we've been glorifying body-death as the medium for inheritance *more* than Christ.

This might be *unusual* to you. I've stopped putting the unusual past God, especially after seeing *Planet Earth: Oceans*. I mean, c'mon. Those translucent creatures are an actual freak-show. God has some quirk. He might even have a line of pink running through His Southern-Baptist hair, which would look pretty *bold* on His middle eastern Jewish body.

The controversy surrounding this is simply *timing*. Everyone believes we're made for heaven. But talk about cashing in on our *"heavenly citizenship"* before you go limp, and you've just cracked open a serious can of worms, despite our beloved Bible-authors doing that very thing.

Our most-loved-author Paul admits he vacationed in the third heaven. Beloved John, too. We tend to box-in the Scriptures with: *"That happened then but not now."* Either way, lots of debates are about timing.

"Jesus is coming back at this time!"

"Oh my gosh. I completely disagree. It's at a different time than you said!"

Exit terrible debate.

I've had a few mystical encounters with God myself. It all begins with the movie Avatar. Pocahontas-remake or not, I loved the movie. It's set on the lush alien planet, Pandora. Pandora is basically earth on crack; primitive big-blue-people, terrifying exotic wildlife (like swoll-jumbo-cats with fangs), diverse-beautiful-landscapes including ethereal-floating-mountains and colorful-luminescent-rainforest-cities, an organic underground nature-neural-network, and I have to mention: bird-mounts. Despite said awesomeness, this luscious planet is sexy to Earth for what's underneath: unobtanium ($20 million per unrefined kilogram).

Trigger-happy, cigarette-smoking, greedy Earthers show up on the beautiful planet ready to wage an all-out-war for this precious metal. Meanwhile, their nerd department (scientists) has created Avatars ($5-billion-dollar big-blue-people-suits for humans) with hopes of making peace with the locals. A war-trodden and paralyzed former Marine, Jake Sully, gets to suit-up with the nerds and, while he should be providing intel to the jacked, toxically-masculine Army General, he instead falls in love with a big-blue-woman. Queue epic battle between Earthers and primitive locals. Earth loses despite its grit and massive army. Jake gets the girl and gets to enjoy a permanently, non-paralyzed big-blue-body. This is my summary of Avatar.

I've always loved *"other-worlds"* since I was a kid. (I am nerdy, and I like it.) Most of my childhood was spent immersed in various digital worlds (video games): included, but not limited to, EverQuest, Dark Age of Camelot, and World of Warcraft. To a wide-eyed geek like me, these massive multiplayer online role-playing games (MMORPG's) were all epic worlds asking to be explored, and they consumed my life. When I divorced the computer at nineteen—*I wept.* For one, I actually loved my nerdy friends. And two, I would miss the adventure.

Eight years post-video-game-addiction, and I'm at Legacy Discipleship School in Dadeville, Alabama. Francois Fineberg (one of the world's best, unknown teachers) had just invited us all to spend quality time with God. I found a couch long enough to hold my body and sprawled out. I thought to myself, *"I wonder what's for lunch."* Add a million other random thoughts, and my *QT with Jesus* was me unable to hold a conversation. That's typical.

Once I realized my mind was annoyingly racing, I intentionally centered my heart and my thoughts on Jesus. It's like looking someone in the eyes and putting away your phone. I began imagining Him, with the eyes of my heart, healing whole towns as explained in the Gospels. I looked to Him on the Cross buying my Shalom. I pictured Him rising from the dead in golden-glory. This is just filling your mind with thoughts of Jesus via your God-given imagination.

And then: the world grew strangely dim, and I saw Jesus staring at me with a big smile. He had smile lines. The way He carried Himself was Honor personified; perfect purity and Kingliness. His holiness made me question if I, little ole me, ought to draw close, and yet the love in His eyes beckoned me closer. Just from His non-verbals: He knew everything about me and still loved me. I consented and... *well, Jesus kissed me on the lips.*

That might be too much for you. It was for me too. At that moment, though, it was as if perversion no longer existed. I completely forgot, if just for a moment, about anything other than true Love. His touch was the safest thing I had ever felt. He was perfectly pure, and there was not even a shadow of evil in Him. He reached out His hand and asked, *"Do you want to come with Me?"* Again, in my heart, I gave a *yes*. We walked to a circular grove of trees. In the very center stood a familiar site: the blue-fruit-tree from Avatar.

Of all the things in the movie that stuck with me the most—*it was that fruit tree.* When I first saw Jake Sully bite into that gushy-alien-fruit at the local theatre, I thought to myself, *"Why is Pandora so much better than Earth? God, you created*

Earth, and some random dude created this." That's kind of rude, to be honest. But that's exactly what I thought. I never told a soul. And, yet, here I am years later, with the eyes of my heart, alongside Jesus in a grove of trees staring at a Pandoran tree. I looked at Jesus and thought, *"Um, what?"* He nodded and threw me a plump blue-fruit. I bit into it, and I heard in my heart: *"I know everything you've ever thought about. I was there with you at the theatre. Even the moments you don't remember, I still think about them. I've always known you wanted to taste this. And I know you've longed for other worlds—that is from Me. You're going to be pleasantly surprised."*

This is weird. But it spoke my language. I knew in boyish wonder: *"No mind can comprehend the things God is preparing for us."* Perhaps its epic, earth-like planets to discover more of Him. Maybe that's why the universe is so big. Maybe that's one piece of the pie of what we'll do for eternity. I would be so down for that to be a thing. All of creation is groaning, and that includes more than earth.

Something changed in me after that moment—*I became much more physically affectionate.* I have always felt uncomfortable in my own skin since I was a small boy. From sexual abuse to puberty to growing pains to stretch marks—*I didn't like to be touched.* I realized how much freedom I had experienced when my friends actually asked me to stop love-scratching their back during prayer. (You know: the back rub with your fingernails). *"My bad."*

I learned there is a beautiful, holy familial, physical affection that belongs to brothers and sisters in the family of God. So many things, namely perversion, tries to steal this sweetness. Fresh off a kiss from Jesus, I remember seeing all the girls at that school with so much purity. It was like I was their Pops, and they were my sweet, little girlies.

Up until then, I hugely struggled to feel loved and known by other people. One of the biggest reasons was because I give and express love through healthy physical affection, and that expression had been robbed from me. This is a sweet way of saying that Jesus enjoys restoring the soul. It's His luxurious love that restores our soul.

When I share stories like this, I normally go out of my way to communicate my love for the Word of God. The Scriptures are my rails (but also open your eyes to the wildness in them). Growing up in conservative, academic Christianity, there is a taboo surrounding the experiential, despite the Scriptures triumphantly advocating a knowledge by experience.

To me, it's not one or the other. Jesus, in fact, was pretty swimming in both. Before Jesus ever performed a miracle, the actual-blue-sky opened up, and audibly God spoke: *"This is my beloved Son in whom I am well pleased"* (insert Morgan Freeman's voice). Doves were involved. I wish the Scriptures included peripheral dialogue of the people watching this mystical Jesus moment. I would imagine the Jerusalem drug-rats thought they had eaten one too many mushrooms.

After this mountain-top experience, Jesus is *"taken by the Holy Spirit"* into the desert where he fasts from food and is tested by a fallen angel named Lucifer, also known as Satan, *"The Accuser."* In all three conversations between Jesus and this used-to-be angel, you hear a recurring refrain: *"If you are the Son of God, perform!"*

Notice it's deceivingly similar to what God the Father had just spoken to Jesus days before. *"This is My beloved Son."*

The subtle differences are huge. Satan excluded the word *"Beloved."* Love casts out fear, and fear is the Dark Side's only tactic. It would be self-deprecating for Satan to assure you of God's love. *Knowing* you are God's beloved is a powerful weapon in your hand. The other difference might be the most common temptation known to man: *perform to become.* While the Father said, *"This is my Son,"* the accuser said, *"If you are, prove it."* Colossians says, *"Let no one deceive you"* with thinking that opposes *"You are complete in Christ."*

Identity cannot birth from performance. But performance will birth from your identity. When we try to prove who we are by what we do, we deny what God has already said is true about us. Our job is to rest in who God says we are. You can do *everything* in the Christian life *for* acceptance or *from* acceptance, and this distinction is the difference between life and death.

So, what did Jesus do? You would think after His recent mystical encounter with God that Jesus would've been like: *"Uh, hey Luci. I literally just heard God say I was already His Son, and He loves me. He straight opened the skies and said it like a few seconds ago. So, you can kindly buzz off."* Jesus probably isn't that sassy. I added the sass.

How did Jesus respond? The *written* Word. Jesus chose to stand on the written promises of God in the Scriptures for His spiritual warfare. Again, He made this choice *right after* having an epic, mountain-top experience with God. Imagine if He leaned on His experience. It would disqualify us to repeat the pattern! With every fresh temptation, we might just roll over and say, *"Well, I haven't heard an audible voice or had a cray-cray out-of-body spirit-rave, so I guess you're right Satan."*

Fortunately for us, as Paul says in Galatians, *"We are children of promise."* Wield the promises in the written Word that the Holy Spirit has quickened in your heart as your spiritual warfare. One of my most favorite: *"Having been justified by faith, we have peace with God through our Lord Jesus Christ, through Whom we also have access by faith, into this grace, in which we stand"* (Rom. 5:1).

I'm righteous. I have peace with God. I have full access. It's all through Christ. It's in the Word. These are weapons for you to wield every time someone or something yells the opposite.

As for experience: I think encounters with God are like epic date nights. Bring on the wine and pleasantries. I am *so* in. Relationships are experiential in nature. You'd never make babies if you just knew facts about your wife and never ventured to *experience* her. I could write a half-decent book detailing the swirly highlights of my relationship with Jesus. But it is my opinion that strong relationships are built on the enjoyment of one another in the everyday *mundane*. Grocery-shopping-covenant-glory.

Beloved, you don't need epic tales or swirls of feelings to know or enjoy God. When I think about my relationship with God, my favorite part is the normal, non-epic goofiness. I would rather have quiet confidence and enjoyment than anything else.

"You make God laugh" was the first prophetic word I ever received. I'm content giggling with Jesus. No wild exploit, no goosebumps, no levitation needed, just simple enjoyment of God. And if, as I'm growing in friendship with Him, weird things happen, I'll hold on to His hand and trust His heart is good.

PROMPTS

Daddy-Daughter-Dates

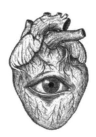

Ask the Holy Spirit to tell you what His favorite part about your personality is. He made you and knows you very well. And you are *very* good.

Selah.

My brothers have many daughters. They are sweet, little nuggets. They are similar and also wildly unique. Their ideal day, their likes and dislikes, their personality, and the way they receive love: *they are all nuanced and different.*

Fathers learn their daughters and intentionally connect with them. These are like specially crafted daddy-daughter-dates. What might be one daughter's dream is another's nightmare. It takes relationship to know *how* to connect. The Lord wants to do this with you. Don't quiet the Lord's voice in you that speaks to very specific, intimate moments about your personhood or past. Take a moment, connect your heart to God, and let the Holy Spirit fill your imagination with Fatherly affection.

Selah.

Begin dwelling on Christ, seated in heavenly places, at the right hand of the Father. You're there *in* Christ. Let your imagination fill with glory.

Selah.

What are some promises in the written Word that the Holy Spirit has quickened to you? *"That hasn't happened to me."* This can be as simple as a verse *"sticking out"* to you or a warm sense of peace as you are reading. These highlighted promises of God should become the banner of your life. When outward things, like people and experiences, seem to say the opposite of what God has promised, above all things, guard your heart from believing anything else. Have you strayed from leaning your weight on His words? This is how discouragement takes root in our lives. Return to your new-natural state of living by God's promises. Let His words be continually on your lips. Write them on your mirror and visit them every day.

Selah.

SPACE FOR YOU

Record the mountain-top or mundane.

LYRICS

Listen to: Diamonds As Your Skin

Diamonds as Your skin
Colors I can't describe
Oil runs down all over You
Clouds surrounding Your glory
And away, away a waterfall flowing down
In gold to a pond of red
It's bubbling, bubbling, bubbling
Your heart is exploding

I am loved
I am holy and righteous
I am placed above
By the blood of Jesus
Seated in Heaven

Kingly is Your smile
Affections I can't deny
Love runs through Your thoughts for me
Your eyes are drawing me into You
And away, away we go to the
City of Your love: Jerusalem

It's hovering, hovering and buzzing
All the saints are singing, singing, singing, singing

I am loved
I am holy and righteous
I am placed above
By the blood of Jesus
Seated in Heaven

Seated in heaven
Seated in heaven
Seated in heavenly places
Seated in heavenly places

Chapter Thirteen
LOVE SECRETS

My sweet mom, Joy, played piano for churches all over the East Coast. My cheeks got pinched by so many old ladies. *Pray for my face.* I was always with my mom. There I was, toddler John Mark, in the church pew of nearly every denomination and, like a kid at an ice cream shop, I sampled all the church flavors. You guess which one is Vanilla—*just kidding.*

The first time I experienced the swirly rainbow flavor of church, the pastor interrupted the service and had mom get on her knees in the center of the sanctuary. A serious-faced group surrounded her and started shouting in a foreign language. She looked tense and uncomfortable. It was weird.

Then the pastor bossed her around, *"Start speaking in tongues!"* It was forceful. He *literally* opened her mouth with his hands. Then it was judgmental; apparently, she wasn't a Christian because she couldn't speak their strange language. I had no idea what was happening, but I knew one thing: no, thank you. Get your rainbow hands away from my Mom, dude.

Kids are the best receivers of information and the worst interpreters of it. From that moment, I decided the Holy Spirit and anyone who operated in His gifts were unsafe people, and *"that whole deal"* was definitely not for me.

On top of the rainbow swirl, I was indoctrinated to believe *"those people"* were operating under the influence of the demonic. Or maybe they were just emotionally charged crazies with no self-respect. I basically agreed after having a front-row seat to the shenanigans.

I'd like to recognize the mindset I adopted was judgmental and narrow. One crappy slice of pizza can't possibly indict all Italians. Or, more importantly: pizza. I let one rotten experience determine my mindset, and that bad apple robbed me from the healthy version. Pain typically jumps to bad conclusions.

Despite my conservative-induced prejudice and rainbow-scars, the Holy Spirit encountered me in my janky Accord at the age of 24. With just one bear-hug, He effectively ruined my safe-but-also-not-fruitful systematic theology. And guess what. The Holy Spirit is the least-controlling Person *ever*. If I would not, He would not.

His invitation into relationship was love, not force. I could say no without punishment but, *"The love of God [was] shed abroad in [my] heart, by the Holy Spirit"* (Rom. 5:5). And so, I consented. That one *yes* did more in my heart than a lifetime of sensible-but-dead Christian religion. I left that Wal-Mart parking lot with a bit more than staples.

My heart softened to the Holy Spirit, and lots of good things happened. The first thing I noticed was that the Scriptures opened up in a new, magical way. And *boy, oh, boy*. I remember slowly blinking a lot, generally being mind-blown, and frequently spouting, *"What in the actual world."* Serious scales fell off my eyes, and all the ooey-gooey New Covenant realities of Jesus' *finished* work founded me. I became convinced of my acceptance.

The second thing I noticed was His heart and voice for other people. I still remember the first time I heard, *"I want to heal that lady's back."* I responded in my head, *"Um, okay. I'm in a gas station. I have no idea who that is."* After an internal, kind-of-hilarious dialogue, I prayed for her and the back pain left. This was the first time I ever saw healing. *"Is this the first healing since Jesus?"*

Every prominent Christian voice I had previously been allowing influence in my heart vilified God as the sickness-giver/allower. And yet, as I began hearing the Holy Spirit's voice in everyday life, He only ever wanted to heal. Since that day, I've seen the miraculous countless times in the most mundane of situations. And just so you know, I've said *no* many, many times to the Holy Spirit's invitation to breakthrough. Whether it's fear of what people would think or lack of compassion, it's always been a cringy *no* from me that looks like giving the silent treatment to God. Luckily: His invitations don't change based on our RSVP. I've said *yes* many times too.

The third thing I noticed was the desire to speak in tongues. There was such a mysterious, confusing fog surrounding this whole *tongues* thing. Even the word triggered me after such a gnarly experience. Also: I thought it sounded stupid and annoying—*just being honest.* Yet, the desire for it came from the Holy Spirit.

I remember saying, *"Can you teach me what the deal is with tongues?"* Tongues, as defined from here forward, is specifically: a heavenly prayer language from God. For this, I waited an eternity for God to take control of my mouth and *do it already.* I thought I'd lose control, maybe levitate a little bit, get fat-goosebumps and then receive downloads Matrix-style of a new dope language.

Turns out, the Holy Spirit's gentleness applies to tongues. Recurring news flash: God is not an overpowering control-freak. If I would not, He would not. He can. He's God. But He's Love and enjoys loving relationships where our consent is considered. When I asked the Holy Spirit, He would say something to the effect of, *"Start speaking by faith."* I was waiting for Him to take control of me. He was waiting for me to start speaking by faith. Awkward. That might be the epitome of an unrenewed mind.

When I finally uttered what seemed like nonsense, it was anticlimactic. *"What am I saying? Also, why is this a thing?"* I didn't know if what I was saying was real or what it was accomplishing—*if anything.* After excavating the Scriptures, it clicked for me. *"For if I pray in a tongue [heavenly language], my spirit prays, but my mind is unfruitful"* (1 Cor. 14:14). Our mind is not fruitful means: we don't understand the language we're speaking. I thought once I started speaking in tongues, I would always comprehend the words with my mind.

"What about interpretation?" This was a huge hang-up for me too. In short: Paul was specifically correcting public

gatherings [*"If the whole church comes together in one place"* *(1 Cor. 14:23)*] where everyone prayed in tongues to the point that no known language was *ever* spoken and *"the unbelievers and uninformed"* never even knew what was happening. No one heard the Good News. Not cool, bro. *Privately,* Paul spoke in tongues more than all of the Corinthians combined but would have rather spoken five words in a known language than ten thousand words in tongues *publicly* (1 Cor. 14:18).

This distinction between private tongues and public tongues is why Paul could say, *"I wish you all spoke in tongues"* (1 Cor. 14:5) to the Corinthian church. Quick break: Paul wished *everyone* in the church spoke in tongues. We don't tend to believe this because he says chapters before, *"Do all speak with tongues? Do all interpret?"* (1 Cor. 12:30). We assume the answer is *no,* when Paul answers with: *"If you don't, then desire to."*

Simply put: *every* believer is invited to speak in private tongues. This private prayer language is available to all, and *you* choose with *your will* when to pray. Paul said, *"I will pray with my spirit"* (1 Cor. 14:15). We do *not* need to wait on God to pray in private tongues. The free-will that is involved here is obvious since the Corinthians needed training on how to operate in this gift with honor. The Spirit wasn't *making* them do it wrong. Side-note: Crazy homeless Joe and Karen from accounting might willfully express this gift differently. You don't have to be *cray-cray* or forfeit normalcy and personality. The Holy Spirit, just like Jesus, has power, love, and a *sound mind.*

Whereas private tongues are available to all and can be expressed without restraint, not every believer is invited to speak in public tongues, which has the specific purpose of being interpreted in a known language for the building up of the gathered church. This gift of public tongues functions *"as the Lord determines"* (1 Cor. 12:11). Paul advocated the heavenly prayer language function this way in church gatherings because tongues, *without interpretation*, only build yourself up. He was being mindful of others.

My paraphrase: *"Don't just pray in tongues to God the whole time when you gather together. You're all just building yourself up, and not being mindful of others. Each of you has a hymn, or word of instruction, or revelation, or a tongue with interpretation to offer the body (1 Cor. 14:26). There should be peace, not confusion. Whoever is speaking and has everyone's attention, if he speaks in tongues, give space for an interpretation, so the people listening can be edified."*

The order Paul instituted for interpretation often becomes legalistic today. When I used to think this way, I remember hearing someone barely speak in tongues during worship at church and cringed, *"Ahhh! I'm melting!"* Just because you hear tongues doesn't mean it's wrong or out of place. Tongues *"does not speak to men but to God"* (1 Cor. 14:2). For example, worship is *towards* God, not men. If you hear someone's worship, it's not *for* you, but you can join in your own worship *towards* God. The heart of tongue-interpretation was to ensure *everyone* was edified, in a known language, when the church came together.

Side-note: many use tongues as a platform to condemn. I experienced this first-hand. *"If you don't speak our weird language, you're not saved."* Sounds like *The Accuser* to me. You can take that weird pressure off. Jesus' blood saves you, beloved. Everything upon this foundation is an invitation to *more*. Love always invites. And hey: you can kindly reject this invitation if you'd like.

Paul addresses private versus public tongues, but also gives our greatest insight into practically, how tongues work: *"My spirit prays."* What do we know about our spirit in light of what Christ has done? *"He who is joined to the Lord is one spirit with Him"* (1 Cor. 6:17). Everything works when you build from our mystical, holy union with God. Tongues, a Biblically defined non-earthly prayer language, is the Holy Spirit, Himself, praying *in us*. We co-labor with Him by letting Him use our voice!

It was awkward for a long time not understanding in English what I was praying, even though the Scriptures explicitly describe this language's operation as: *"My mind is not fruitful."* The Western world worships the mind. We tend to *hate* tongues. This childlike gift makes brain-heavy control-freaks, *freak* out.

While we hate the fact that our mind isn't fruitful, it's actually the most beneficial aspect of the language. *"The Spirit joins to help us in our weakness [which is] we do not know what we ought to pray for and the Spirit Himself intercedes for us with groanings [words too glorious for a known language]"* (Rom. 8:26). Why the unfruitful mind? Because we don't know what *or* how we ought to pray. If I'm honest with my prayer life: *"I have no idea how to pray for this."* I've also prayed a lot of carnal prayers. Even Garth Brooks is thankful for unanswered prayers he prayed in English.

Tongues bypass the mind and allow the Holy Spirit, who knows all things, to pray for us! We get to sit back and trust that whatever He's praying—*that it's good, it's for us, and exactly what we need.* This is a beautiful faith exercise. It's also a brilliant move by God. He's placed the authority of life and death on *our* tongue (Prov. 18:21).

This lavish authority is magnified in light of Christ's finished work, which has made us a royal priesthood (1 Pet. 2:9). We give lip service to this phrase, but it holds great power. *"And the priest shall set a value, whether good or bad; as you, the priest, value it, so it shall be"* (Levi. 27:12). Christ is our High Priest and calls *you* the priest of your home. Priests determine value, good or bad, with their *words*.

You're also married to the King of Kings. Your Husband has all authority and power and, *"where the word of a King is, there is power"* (Eccl. 8:4). When you speak, royal-beloved, you are always creating life or death. Jesus' half-brother James compared the tongue—*what we say*—to the rudder on a ship, saying, *"The tongue is a small member, yet it boasts of great things"* (James 3:5). Bridled words can beautifully enrich our life. An untamed tongue will set a destructive fire to it.

Whenever God speaks, His words bring life because there is no darkness in Him. The Lord, wanting us to live, said to *"meditate on His words day and night."* This *"meditate"* renders, *"mutter under your breath."* When *you* say what God has said, you choose life. *"For [my words] are life to those that find them, and health to all their flesh"* (Prov 4:22).

We can say what God has said in our known language; that would be speaking *"with our understanding"* in English. You, being a temple, could view this as *from* your soul; the inner courts. The inner courts were also known as *The Holy Place.* We can also let the Holy Spirit *in* us, speak in His language; that would be speaking *"with our spirit"* in tongues. You, being a temple, could view this as *from* your spirit; the Holy of Holies. The Holy of Holies was also known as *The Most Holy Place.* *"But you, beloved, building yourselves up on your Most Holy faith, praying in the Holy Spirit, keep yourself in the love of God"* (Jude 1:20). Whether we speak the words of God from our soul or spirit, *both* are holy.

The Scriptures give beautiful insights into the weighty glory of what is actually happening when we *"pray in the Holy Spirit."* When we pray in tongues, we repair our emotional world and physical body (1 Cor. 14:4). Modern science is just now discovering the depth of brain plasticity. Entire centers of your brain respond to your words. Every cell in your body has response-technology. Death can be seen under a microscope in the cellular structure just moments after dwelling on *bitter* memories. And vice-versa. Cell-formation is beautiful and impeccable when dwelling on good things. *"Whatever is true, whatever is noble, whatever is right, whatever is pure, whatever is lovely, whatever is admirable—if anything is excellent or praiseworthy—think about such things"* (Phil. 4:8). This could campaign well for positive self-talk. Imagine the life-giving glory of what the Holy Spirit is saying when you lend your mouth to Him.

There are more nuggets. When we pray in tongues, we give thanks well (1 Cor. 14:17). When we pray in tongues, we speak the mysteries (love secrets) of God (1 Cor. 14:2). When we pray in tongues, the Holy Spirit, Himself, is interceding for all believers in perfect accordance with God's will (Rom. 8:27). While you might pray in English for a ring by spring, when you pray in tongues: The Holy Spirit could be advocating for your spouse by name, your marriage, your family, and your future.

With a Scriptural basis for how tongues operated as well as the language's content and purpose, I started singing in the language all the time. Knowing the Holy Spirit *in me* was praying warmed my heart with the reality of Holy-Spirit-oneness. After the first few months of praying in tongues, I noticed an ease and sweetness. Because I was able to pray without having to engage my mind, I was actually praying without ceasing! I also noticed a massive increase of *all* the other Holy Spirit gifts. It seemed like a *"fanning of the flame."*

Generally, I don't ask for an interpretation to my private tongue. I just believe by faith all the nuggets in the Word are indeed happening. I've received an interpretation a few times and it's always been a *knowing*, as opposed to a word-for-word translation. My favorite: I *knew*, just in this instance, I was praying protection over a family in the underground church in China. I was being my normal goofy self on a morning drive to church, nonchalantly praying in the Spirit, when all of a sudden: great, big love hit my heart for a family across the globe in China. I felt an urgency to *"cover them in prayer"* with my heavenly prayer language which finally released after an almost all-day prayer-sesh. Based on the Word, I knew that the Holy Spirit *in me* was interceding for them in perfect accordance with God's heart. It was an honor to be the mouthpiece for it.

This child-like prayer language has become a simple part of my normal Christian life and is how most of my music is born. I constantly rotate between English and this heavenly prayer language in times of worship and songwriting. *"So, what shall I do? I will pray with my spirit, but I will also pray with my understanding; I will sing with my spirit, but I will also sing with my understanding"* (1 Cor. 14:15).

I'm so glad my heart softened to the Holy Spirit. I've learned He is our Great Collaborator and enjoys imbuing our words with weight and power. He has *"guided me into the experiential knowledge of Christ"* (John 16:13). He is not a spirit of fear, but He exudes and shares with us agape love, the strength and power of God, and an anchoring mental clarity (2 Timothy 1:7). He is wonderfully sweet and a fine best-friend.

Life with the Holy Spirit turns boring Christianity into a magical Narnia land where anything is possible. Soften up to the Spirit and you just might explore your own *love secrets*.

PROMPTS

Spirit-Sweetie

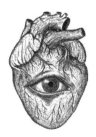

Have you ever opened your heart to friendship with the Holy Spirit? He's a sweetie. He is, in every way, like Jesus. He's the Spirit of Christ *in* us. He loves revealing Jesus to us. It's His *favorite* thing to do. Take a few moments and ask the Holy Spirit to become your dearest friend.

Selah.

Like Paul, I desire for you to pray in heavenly languages which is actually for *your* benefit. *"For whoever prays in an unknown tongue builds himself up"* (1 Cor. 14:4). If you've never prayed in tongues, you can if you desire to. Let me pray for you.

Holy Spirit, I pray You would come upon this sweet brother or sister reading these words and help them to start operating in the gift of tongues. I pray that You shed abroad the love of the Father clearly in their hearts and saturate them in Your power. Amen. Start speaking by faith in heavenly languages. Trust that the Holy Spirit is praying good things.

Selah.

You can ask for an interpretation of what He's saying. Or, you can just believe by faith that what He's praying is for your benefit. Write down anything you hear.

Selah.

Finish by connecting your heart to God, focusing your thoughts on Christ, and enjoying God's love.

Selah.

SPACE FOR YOU

Ink the Holy Spirit vibes.

LYRICS

Listen to: Love Secrets + Sweeter Than Wine

You are one with me
Singing love secrets
Love secrets over me

You are one with me
Singing love secrets
Singing love secrets
C'mon love secrets

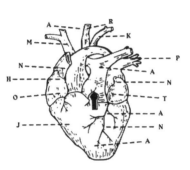

TALK TO ME

Jesus is pretty great, yeah? He's a fine hubby. And, He's just imitating His Pops. Thanks for teaching us these things, Holy Spirit. How fun for us to be a part of this happy union. We're just getting started too. There are worlds left to discover of our eternal Lord. I'm pretty excited about that.

I hope you've experienced the Father, the Son, and the Holy Spirit through this book. I would love to hear everything that happened. You can reach out to me on Instagram: @johnmarkpantana or email me: hello@johnmarkpantana.com.

Also, how incredible was the art in this book? It was lovingly crafted by Daniel Neuman. You can find him on Instagram under @daniel_neuman. Recommend ten-out-of-ten.

ABOUT THE AUTHOR

Well, if you've read the book, I've shared lots of myself with you. I'll add some *random factoids*:

I am 6 foot 5. I identify more with goofy white boy than musician or author. I learned how to ride a bike when I was 27. It makes me happy. I was escorted to jail for three days, where I did, in fact, gamble some blueberry muffins. Don't drive 100 miles per hour.

I am obsessed with British accents. I've seen all the food documentaries and, although I really can't kick Chick-Fil-A, I'm a health nerd who reads labels. I like to cook all the things. I dream of having a plot of earth with lots of goats and chickens and humans. My life goal is to enjoy Jesus and follow His peace every day.

Visit my website: www.johnmarkpantana.com for music, chord charts, blog, merch, and more.

Made in the USA
Columbia, SC
02 March 2021

33815185R00100